Religious Epistemology

ROYAL INSTITUTE OF PHILOSOPHY SUPPLEMENT: 81

EDITED BY

Stephen Law

CAMBRIDGE
UNIVERSITY PRESS

CAMBRIDGE
UNIVERSITY PRESS

Shaftesbury Road, Cambridge CB2 8EA, United Kingdom

One Liberty Plaza, 20th Floor, New York, NY 10006, USA

477 Williamstown Road, Port Melbourne, VIC 3207, Australia

314–321, 3rd Floor, Plot 3, Splendor Forum, Jasola District Centre, New Delhi – 110025, India

103 Penang Road, #05–06/07, Visioncrest Commercial, Singapore 238467

Cambridge University Press is part of Cambridge University Press & Assessment, a department of the University of Cambridge.

We share the University's mission to contribute to society through the pursuit of education, learning and research at the highest international levels of excellence.

www.cambridge.org
Information on this title: www.cambridge.org/9781108453257

A catalogue record for this publication is available from the British Library

ISBN   978-1-108-45325-7   Paperback

Contents

Notes on Contributors

CHARITY ANDERSON

Charity Anderson is Assistant Professor of Philosophy at Baylor University.

MICHAEL BERGMANN

Michael Bergmann is Professor of Philosophy at Purdue University.

JOHN COTTINGHAM

John Cottingham is Professor Emeritus of Philosophy at Reading University, Professorial Research Fellow at Heythrop College London, Professor of Philosophy of Religion, University of Roehampton, and an Honorary Fellow of St John's College Oxford. He is an authority on Descartes and translator of his works, and has also published widely on moral philosophy and philosophy of religion. His recent books include The Spiritual Dimension (CUP), Cartesian Reflections (OUP), How to Believe (Bloomsbury), and Philosophy of Religion: Towards a More Humane Approach (CUP).

JOHN HAWTHORNE

John Hawthorne is Professor of Philosophy at the University of Southern California.

YOAAV ISAACS

Yoaav Isaacs is Research Assistant Professor of Philosophy at the University of North Carolina at Chapel Hill.

STEPHEN LAW

Stephen Law is Reader in Philosophy at Heythrop College, University of London.

doi:10.1017/S1358246117000327   © The Royal Institute of Philosophy and the contributors 2017
Royal Institute of Philosophy Supplement **81** 2017

Notes on Contributors

JUSTIN MCBRAYER

Justin McBrayer is Associate Professor of Philosophy at Fort Lewis College, the public liberal arts college for the state of Colorado. He works largely in ethics and philosophy of religion.

DUNCAN PRITCHARD

Duncan Pritchard is Chancellor's Professor of Philosophy at UCIrvine, USA, and Professor of Philosophy at the University of Edinburgh, UK. His recent monographs include Epistemological Disjunctivism (Oxford UP, 2012) and Epistemic Angst: Radical Skepticism and the Groundlessness of Our Believing (Princeton UP, 2015).

ALEXANDER R. PRUSS

Alexander Pruss is Professor of Philosophy at Baylor University.

J. L. SCHELLENBERG

J. L. Schellenberg is Professor of Philosophy at Mount Saint Vincent University and Adjunct Professor in the Faculty of Graduate Studies at Dalhousie University. His present research is focused on the consequences of human immaturity for how we do philosophy.

Three Ways to Improve Religious Epistemology

J. L. SCHELLENBERG

Abstract

Religious epistemology is widely regarded as being in a flourishing condition. It is true that some very sharp analytical work on religion has been produced by philosophers in the past few decades. But this work, for various cultural and historical reasons, has been kept within excessively narrow bounds, and the result is that the appearance of flourishing is to a considerable extent illusory. Here I discuss three important ways in which improvements to this situation might be made.

In this paper I will identify three ways in which religious epistemology remains excessively narrow in its concerns, and three corresponding ways in which this important area of philosophical endeavour might be improved.

1. Beyond Naturalism and Theism

Religious epistemologists have the task of looking at both religious and nonreligious perspectives on the world, considering whether and how we can determine who's right, along with a host of other more detailed but related questions about knowledge as well as justified or reasonable belief or faith concerning religious matters. But in practice only two perspectives have become salient: *theism*, which says that there is a God upholding nature, a creator of heaven and earth who possesses all power, knowledge, and goodness, and *scientific naturalism*, which holds, to the contrary, that reality is a single unified system structured by natural laws, which science is working successfully to expose. Each tends to be treated as exhausting the category – religious or nonreligious – to which it belongs. Accordingly, religious epistemologists who thought they had learned that scientific naturalism is false would be inclined to infer that theism is true, and thus to say that belief of theism is epistemically justified for them or can even count as knowledge. Similarly, those who concluded that *theism* is false would be inclined to infer that *scientific naturalism* is true, and thus to say that

doi:10.1017/S1358246117000273

1

belief of scientific naturalism is epistemically justified for them or can even count as knowledge.[1]

But these are inclinations that, if followed, can lead only into rather large errors. Let 'R' stand for 'Some religious possibility is actualized,' 'NON-R' for 'Some nonreligious possibility is actualized,' 'T' for theism, 'SN' for scientific naturalism, '→' for logical entailment, and '~' for negation. Then it is correct to write

$$T \rightarrow \sim SN$$

and also (because it logically follows) correct to write

$$SN \rightarrow \sim T.$$

In words: if theism is true then scientific naturalism is false, and if scientific naturalism is true then theism is false. Furthermore, it may quite properly be said that

$$T \rightarrow \sim (R \ \& \ \sim T)$$

and also that

$$SN \rightarrow \sim (NON\text{-}R \ \& \ \sim SN).$$

In words: if theism is true then religious truth can't be realized in any *other and incompatible* way, and if scientific naturalism is true, then non-religious truth can't be realized in any *other and incompatible* way. But it would be a mistake to claim that

$$\sim T \rightarrow SN$$

or (therefore) to affirm what logically follows from that claim by contraposition:

$$\sim SN \rightarrow T.$$

In words: the falsehood of theism does not entail the truth of scientific naturalism, nor therefore does the falsehood of scientific naturalism entail the truth of theism. Of course, if someone did a lot more work than any philosopher has yet done to rule out *other* ways in which R could be true and *other* ways in which NON-R could be true, these results *together* with ~T might legitimately be

---

[1] For representative discussion, see Daniel C. Dennett and Alvin Plantinga, *Science and Religion: Are They Compatible?* (Oxford: Oxford University Press, 2011).

said to entail SN. Similarly for $\sim$ SN $\rightarrow$ T. But given present circumstances of inquiry, we who are not religious apologists or scientific activists but philosophical investigators have to leave open, as a matter for further inquiry, that

$$R \;\&\; (\sim SN \;\&\; \sim T)$$

as well as that

$$NON\text{-}R \;\&\; (\sim SN \;\&\; \sim T).$$

In words: it could well be, there is no justification to deny, that the religion category gets things right while *both* of the views claiming all our attention today – both scientific naturalism and theism – are false, or else that the *non*-religion category gets things right while both are false. Now wouldn't *that* be interesting!

Yes, it would. But it is an interesting possibility to which most contemporary religious epistemology is closed by virtue of assuming to be true the claims that I have here suggested are *erroneously* assumed in the present context of inquiry about things religious.

Of course some will resist that suggestion. One way to try this would involve an appeal to the interconnectedness of philosophical concerns over time. Philosophers like other inquirers, so it may be said, do not rightly ignore the concerns of those who went before, or rightly pass up a chance to fulfil an agenda set by other philosophers years ago if such a chance comes along. And perhaps this is how well known Christian philosophers such as Alvin Plantinga are inclined to view their situation. But it's one thing to vigorously defend a theistic option and look nowhere else for religious ideas – as, say, Gottfried Leibniz and Samuel Clarke did in the seventeenth century – when theistic belief pervades the culture and is at the very least a live option for everyone in philosophy, and quite another to do so when your view is, in relation to philosophy as a whole, at best an outlier and when your main motive for defending it is non-philosophical. Arguably the latter is the Plantinga situation. Leibniz and Clarke themselves, if resurrected in our midst and as truth-intoxicated as we tend to imagine, might recommend to Christian philosophers that they drop 'Christian' from the label with which they identify, philosophically.[2]

---

[2]   For defense of the view that bias infects contemporary philosophy of religion, see Paul Draper and Ryan Nichols, 'Diagnosing Bias in Philosophy of Religion', *The Monist* 96 (2013), 420–446.

J. L. Schellenberg

More generally, if we have seen how philosophical concerns of the past betray shortsightedness or blindness from which we need not suffer, there is no good *philosophical* reason to seek to advance them. Earlier thinkers had little access to the diversity of intellectually sophisticated religious views we now know can be found around the world, and none at all to such recent results of natural science as geological time, which should move us to note how early a position we *may* occupy in (what will be) the total history of inquiry on our planet.[3] Nor did they have the support we have from cognitive science for seeing humans as being, at this early stage, rather biased toward personal representations of divine realities.[4]

Might a theistic philosopher still appropriately say that the metaphysical explanations offered by theism, even if they only represent one small part of conceptual space, are what she is *particularly interested* in exploring, or that theism just seems obvious to her – she cannot help this – and so this is where she is going to *start* when doing philosophy? And might scientific naturalists respond similarly? Perhaps. But then there is still no basis for the assumption, so commonly made, that theism is in any more general way intellectually or philosophically *the only live religious option*, or for offering to the community of inquiry an inference from the falsehood of one of these views to the truth of the other. It's one thing to be working with theism or scientific naturalism or even working *on* making one of these views more resistant to opposition, but it's quite another to treat these two as constituting the only game in town. The game is much larger – or it would be if religious epistemology were properly developed – and theistic philosophers in particular need to reconcile themselves to making a move here or there rather than controlling the board.

Of course, these points, thus baldly stated, may not be sufficient to change many human minds. So let's consider another way of proceeding here, which yields extra confirmation for the idea that religious epistemology should be open to the view that, whatever may be said of R or NON-R, both theism and scientific naturalism are

---

[3] See J. L. Schellenberg, *Evolutionary Religion* (Oxford: Oxford University Press, 2013).
[4] See, for example, Justin L. Barrett, *Why Would Anyone Believe in God?* (Lanham: AltaMira Press, 2004), Pascal Boyer, *Religion Explained: The Evolutionary Origins of Religious Thought* (New York: Basic Books, 2001), and Todd Tremlin, *Minds and Gods: The Cognitive Foundations of Religion* (Oxford: Oxford University Press, 2006).

false. This comes from a consideration of certain *tensions* that exist in both of the popular camps – both in the territory occupied by theism and in that claimed by scientific naturalism – between more familiar and accessible and less familiar and strange ideas.

Take theism first. Here the tension is between the kind and loving – or perhaps harsh and wrathful – *person*-like being many of us learned about at our mother's knee, a being who intervenes in the world and answers prayers, and the more abstract and metaphysically rarefied reality, perhaps outside time altogether, that one might learn about at the knee of Thomas Aquinas. Religious experiences of certain common sorts – sometimes prompted by historical events such as the activities of Jesus of Nazareth – as well as the community life of many vibrant religious traditions will get you the former, and serious theological reflection may lead you to the latter. Prominent theistic religious epistemologists such as Alvin Plantinga, Richard Swinburne, and their acolytes have veered quite close to the person-like God in their reasoning. But they would try to convince you that they can accommodate everything important in the more metaphysically oriented God too. Other theistic philosophers, such as Brian Davies and Keith Ward, would strenuously disagree.

A similar tension exists *within* the personalist conception of the theist's God. For Swinburne and Plantinga would disagree with the sort of process theism that can be linked to the work of Alfred North Whitehead as well as with a view called panentheism, championed by philosophers such as Philip Clayton. And yet all of these views can be – and often are – formulated using the idea of a *divine person*.

So we have some tensions in the theistic camp. But similar tensions exist among scientific naturalists. Here a problem that arises stems from the fact that there are almost as many ways of filling in a naturalistic picture of reality, guided by science, as there are naturalists. Even my broad sketch above might generate quibbles. And of course there can be disagreements among advocates of these various definitions.

But I want to focus on a rather basic and well known tension one finds in this neighborhood, as to whether the science we should look to for our picture of reality is *present* science (represented by available results or those we might achieve from the current methods and assumptions of science over sufficient time) or *ideal* science – science as it might exist in a much more matured and complete and rather different form should scientists have, say, a few hundred thousand years more to plug away. Of course those who hold the former view will resist the latter – for them, in a sense, present science *is* ideal science. But many of those who practice science today would regard this as somewhat over-optimistic, to say the least! Considering what may be required to bridge the divide between quantum theory and general relativity (or to replace those theories with compatible ones), and giving careful attention to how radically different are the basic concepts of quantum physics from any that came before (say, in Newtonian physics), it may seem rather risky to suggest that science with a few hundred thousand years more to work would – assuming the work resulted in whatever advances are needed – look little different from the science we have now. Indeed, it might not seem too much to suggest that even if the world picture of many non-theists, after that much more time and rewarded effort, remained in some sense *naturalistic*, it would stretch our concept of science to the breaking point to call what they had come up with *scientifically* naturalistic.

My aim is not to resolve these tensions between the familiar and the strange (or potentially strange) in theistic and scientifically naturalistic pictures of the world or to suggest that they cannot be resolved, but rather to point out that they are signs of *unfinished business* – certainly just what we might expect if the view I am defending has it right. Even without leaving theism and scientific naturalism we can already observe *variation* within R and NON-R. And we can see the potential for more. Should we really suppose, then, that nothing *other* than theism and scientific naturalism will be revealed to have significance as we transcend the partisan motives that are still so often found among us, and work at ultimate questions a bit longer? Is there really justification to believe that? Here's a thought: it's not because of all we've already learned but because of a lack of humility, and the even broader immaturity of which it is a symptom, that we presently rest content with theism and scientific naturalism in our deliberations. Here's another: if at the *earliest stage* of inquiry we are disposed to think we've come so close to settling the *most profound* matters, it can't be *reason* that gives us this tendency!

Perhaps it will help if at this stage we summarize the reasons that have emerged in our discussion for broadening the discussion in epistemology of religion by moving beyond theism and naturalism to consider other regions represented by R and NON-R. There are basically four reasons. After the first, each strengthens the reason(s) that came before, and together the four make a formidable case.

(1)   Intellectual humility demands a much more modest assessment of what we have so far learned in religious matters.

(2)   Committed scientific naturalists and theists have generally given little or no attention to the investigation of other regions of conceptual space represented by R and NON-R.

(3)   Cognitive science of religion is providing support for the view that humans are specially attracted to agential conceptions of the divine, in such a way as to potentially yield a prejudice against other ways of construing it.

(4)   Finally, and also from science itself, in particular from the contemplation of geological timescales, one learns that if the temporal demands of knowledge on relevant matters for limited intellects are more accurately expressed in *their* terms than in terms of the *human* timeframes we so take for granted, then even in a few thousand years we have barely got started on what would be (were inquiry successful) a long journey perhaps many thousands of times as long as that. Now we have no way of ruling out that the demands of knowledge *are* more accurately thus expressed. Therefore, we have no way of ruling out that we have just got started on the road toward knowledge on religious matters. (This consideration, as noted, strengthens those that came before, but it is also strengthened by them.)

So how should the proposed broadening occur, to make for a genuine improvement? It's clear that we have conceptual diversity, and we need to be open to discovering much more. But the details here might easily get away on us and become unmanageable – perhaps this suggests another motive for analysts who like things crisp and clean to stick to two options! Moreover, we have to make room not only for detailed religious and nonreligious pictures of the world that exist today and are ignored but also for views that haven't yet entered the discussion because they have not yet been *conceived* by limited and immature minds.

My suggestion is that, instead of adding other detailed options to theism and scientific naturalism, we should carve out a larger, more general, more basic religious idea – larger, more general, more basic than theism – that might serve the field of philosophy of religion as a whole, including epistemology of religion, as a sort of *framework* for detailed inquiry. To count, at least in philosophy, as a way in which R could be true, a proposition would need to entail this larger idea. Of course many detailed ideas, including many theisms, would do so. And not just scientific naturalisms, but potentially many different ideas, all those filling the space of NON-R, would count as *ir*religious, and as challenges to religion, by entailing the falsehood of that larger claim. Moreover a variety of other relevant ideas – of religious belief, religious skepticism, religious faith, and so on – might be defined in terms of the more general idea, bringing a heretofore absent *structure* and *organization* to philosophy of religion. By being more general and fundamental, the basic religious claim or proposition or idea would furthermore be much better suited to non-partisan *philosophical* inquiry about religion than traditional theism, and more likely to remain stable, a continuing framework for inquiry that can weather many changes, as we move into the future.

So which general idea should we select? This of course is, and must be, a matter for broad discussion, but I will mention two possibilities, one more general than the other but both more general than theism – either of which, if widely taken up, would mark a signal improvement in how we do philosophy of religion, including religious epistemology. The first, which I have discussed at length elsewhere, I call *ultimism*.[5]

This claim – and it is important to note that 'ultimism' *is* the name of a claim or proposition, not of a proposed new religion – says that there is a triply ultimate reality, a reality ultimate in three ways: metaphysically (in the nature of things), axiologically (in inherent value), and soteriologically (in its value *for us and the world*, that is, in its conduciveness to the attainment by us of an ultimate good). And that's all it says. Nothing here about a divine person who created the world – though notice that that is one way in which the general idea of metaphysical ultimacy could be filled out. Nothing about attributes such as maximal knowledge, power, and love that jointly make for unsurpassable greatness – though notice that that is one way in which we might try to flesh out the more general idea of axiological ultimacy. Nothing, either, about salvation through the appropriate commitment to a personal God – though notice that that is one way in which we might add detail to the more general idea of soteriological ultimicy. Theism, which I have of course just been alluding to, would be regarded as entailing ultimism but ultimism does not entail theism. Theism may represent *one way* in which ultimism could be true, but there are others, maybe very many others. And we could try to determine *what are* these various ways of filling out the claim of ultimism, evaluating them in all the ways that religious epistemology allows. This is how ultimism can provide a better framework for philosophical reflection concerning religion than theism does.

[5] See, for example, J. L. Schellenberg, *Prolegomena to a Philosophy of Religion* (Ithaca: Cornell University Press, 2005).

But ultimism may not be as general or fundamental as things get in the religious domain, when the latter is construed in the manner most likely to benefit philosophy. Elsewhere I have argued that ultimism should, for philosophical purposes, be used to define religion and many other related things. But there are reasons for resisting this view.[6] A more general possibility which I think avoids all such problems as have been mentioned here would focus on the concept of *transcendence* rather than ultimacy. A reality might be transcendent – more than or other than the arena of mundane events or (depending on how it is defined) more than or other than anything physical or natural – and might be transcendent in each of the three ways already suggested, metaphysically, axiologically, and soteriologically, *even if it is not in any respect ultimate.* So we have as a contender for the status of 'basic religious idea of concern to philosophers' the notion of a triply transcendent reality. Out of deference to the repeated 't' in 'triply transcendent,' and with a wink in the direction of theism, we might call the claim that there is such a reality *t-ism.* Both theism and ultimism entail t-ism, but t-ism entails neither of them. Again, we have a broader and better framework for philosophical inquiry concerning religion.

Which more general claim should win out – ultimism, t-ism, or perhaps some notion yet to be introduced to the discussion? I offer no judgment on this here, though I would say that religious epistemology, for reasons set out above, would be much improved by having its inquiries developed within the framework allowed by one of these, rather than by the omnipresent but limiting and error-prone dispute between traditional theism and scientific naturalism. Even naturalists, among those who turn out to have irreligious positions in philosophy of religion, are here allowed to stretch and explore other ways (ways other than scientific naturalism) in which an irreligious perspective on the world might be true. Of course – and this is interesting – naturalists also need to be open to our ways of thinking about the world over time evolving in such a way as to permit the partial or complete erasure of our distinction between the natural and the supernatural. Perhaps 'nature' will one day be conceived in such a way as to be compatible with something like triple transcendence, as then understood. Something similar could happen on the side of theism: perhaps there will be future beings, more intelligent and spiritually sensitive than we, who one day countenance the idea that

[6]   See, for example, Jeanine Diiller, 'The Conceptual Focus of Ultimism: An Object of Religious Concern for the Nones and Somes', *Religious Studies* 49 (2013), 221–233.

J. L. Schellenberg

personal qualities dimly analogous to those which theists now attribute to God represent *one dimension* of a much larger divine reality. Whether on the side of R or Non-R, there may be many more fascinating possibilities in conceptual space than are dreamt of in our present philosophy.

2. Beyond Belief

Religious epistemology as we see it today is limited, hampered, constrained not just by an obsession with naturalism and theism but by its obsession with *believing states* (whether understood categorically or in the graded fashion to be associated with popular talk of 'credences'). As a recent overview of religious epistemology has it, the field is concerned with a variety of theories about whether 'subjects' religious beliefs' can have 'positive epistemic status'.[7] But, you say, don't disbelief and skepticism or doubt also come in for consideration here, at least implicitly? Yes, they do. However notice that disbelief too is belief: if – perhaps because you are a scientific naturalist – you disbelieve that there is a God, you *believe* that there is *no* God. And doubt too has to be understood in terms of belief: if you are in doubt about whether there is a God, then (perhaps among other things) you *neither believe nor disbelieve* that there is a God.

But perhaps it will seem that a focus on these things need not make religious epistemology overly narrow. After all, aren't religious people commonly called *believers*, and aren't epistemologists, in philosophy more generally, concerned with the epistemic status of *beliefs* and with their possible contribution to knowledge and understanding?

To the first question: yes, but if that determines our approach then it is liable again to be shaped by present preoccupations and evaluative concerns – perhaps our own as religious believers or disbelievers – rather than by concern for a generally applicable picture of the field, whose principles religious persons of many different kinds and at many different times might recognize as responding to their situation.

To the second question: yes, these concerns have long been part of general epistemology, but more recently even epistemologists outside philosophy of religion have recognized that we need to be sensitive to the existence and importance of nonbelieving or potentially

[7] Trent Dougherty and Chris Tweedt, 'Religious Epistemology', *Philosophy Compass* (2015) 10: doi: 10.1111/phc3.12185.

nonbelieving cognitive psychological states – states such as the state of *acceptance* explored by L. Jonathan Cohen.[8] Acceptance of the sort Cohen has in mind allows one to take a proposition as a basis for practical and theoretical inference and act on this even when one doesn't believe it, either in the categorical sense of thinking or feeling it to report what is the case or in the graded sense of having some *degree* of belief (perhaps this should rather be called confidence) with respect to it. In this sense one might accept that the prisoner is innocent, or accept that one's spouse is faithful, or accept that a certain path leads out of a cave, or accept that the theory is true while not in any sense believing the relevant proposition – perhaps without having a clue how probable one should say it is. And acceptance of this kind might be but *one* of the nonbelieving cognitive states found in everyday life and inquiry, with which epistemologists (therefore) should concern themselves, along with beliefs.

The two main points I have made here – about believers in religion and belief in epistemology – are connected. For one of the way in which nonbelieving cognitive states could prove their importance is *by showing up in recognizably religious lives.* This possibility should be of great significance for anyone who is intellectually curious, where religious matters are concerned, instead of functioning as an apologist or activist for some particular religious or nonreligious perspective (which stance human nature combined with facts about the nature of religious and irreligious allegiance – in particular *believing* religious and irreligious allegiance – conspire to make all too common even among philosophers). It should be of great significance for anyone thus minded because it might allow religious epistemology to become, at once, more relevant to religion on the ground (which features a goodly share of doubt) and to religion as it may come to exist in the future. If a nonbelieving religious cognitive commitment passes the appropriate epistemological tests whereas believing ones do not, we might even have here a new solution to the old problem of faith and reason.

There are grounds to think that we will find precisely such a disparity between nonbelieving and believing religious commitments, though more discussion is needed to confirm this. Theistic religious epistemologists such as Plantinga and Swinburne have laboured mightily in recent decades to defend the view that traditional theistic and even orthodox Christian beliefs can be epistemically justified or amount to knowledge, despite the sharpest critiques from other

---

[8] See L. Jonathan Cohen, *An Essay on Belief and Acceptance* (Oxford: Clarendon Press, 1992).

orientations – in particular those of scientific naturalists. But there are reasons to locate serious shortcomings both in their approaches and in their results. Our own results in section 1 have a bearing here (section 3 is relevant too, as will become apparent). For even if scientific naturalism – or indeed any present form of naturalism – were provably false, theistic philosophers today would be in no position to infer that any of their religious beliefs are true. More generally, much more investigation than any of us has yet undertaken of religious and non-religious alternatives to views on religion we find attractive would be required to rationally uphold any religious view as a *belief*, given human limitations and immaturity.[9] There is even a new challenge, one that philosophers such as Swinburne and Plantinga have never considered: namely that theism should entail ultimism if it is the religious view it is thought to be *but in fact does not*, since the restriction to a person-like being is at the same time a derogation from axiological ultimacy, which would not be thus restricted.[10] (Of course other religious propositions may not be subject to *this* challenge, and theism does appear to entail t-ism, whatever may be said of its relation to ultimism.)

Now I've already said that such skeptical challenges await further discussion and confirmation or disconfirmation. But suppose they are confirmed. The interesting thing here is this. If our focus in religious epistemology is restricted to religious *beliefs*, then a widely applicable religious skepticism, if borne out by continuing inquiry, would have to be said to mark the end of rational religion. But if religious epistemology is expanded to include a consideration of alternative cognitive states and their evaluation in the ways I have suggested (and am about to suggest), *then it may be just the beginning.*

For suppose that what epistemologists of religion discover, when they develop the broader, more discriminating, and sensitive evaluative criteria needed here, is that a religious faith whose cognitive center is nonbelieving is *much easier to support*, rationally speaking, than are believing forms of faith, in ways that allow even limited, immature humans to rationally have religious faith in response to one religious proposition or another. Perhaps, for example, all that is needed is a simpler or more general proposition than any theistic

---

[9] See J. L. Schellenberg, *The Wisdom to Doubt: A Justification of Religious Skepticism* (Ithaca: Cornell University Press, 2007).
[10] See J. L. Schellenberg, 'God for All Time: From Theism to Ultimism', in Andrei Buckareff and Yujin Nagasawa (Eds.), *Alternative Concepts of God: Essays on the Metaphysics of the Divine* (Oxford: Oxford University Press, 2015).

one, an aim or set of aims – including truth-oriented aims – that is well or uniquely advanced by having religious faith in response to that proposition, and a lack of any good reason to *disbelieve* the proposition. If such were the case, we might be in a position, right now, to supply plenty of epistemic justification for religious faith. But notice: if we had never expanded religious epistemology beyond belief, we would never *know* this.

3. Beyond the Evaluation of Token Responses to Religious Propositions

The third improvement I want to propose requires us to raise our sights from a current preoccupation which may also stem, at least in part, from the partisan or activist orientation that can create an obsession with believing states. This is a preoccupation with whether the religious or nonreligious commitments of *particular people or communities*, usually individuals or communities to be found somewhere in the West today, are rational or epistemically justified or amount to knowledge. Often these people include those doing the inquiry – philosophers may be concerned with whether *they themselves* have achieved a certain epistemic status – and in part because these inquirers are usually religious or nonreligious believers, we tend to find a corresponding focus on particular *believing* commitments.

Again it may seem there is nothing particularly troubling here, at least beyond what we've already discussed in the previous section: isn't it a rather important question for religious epistemology whether (and how) religion or irreligion is, or is not, rational – and this whether it be belief or some other cognitive state that underlies the religious or irreligious stance? Yes, it is. But now it will be necessary to notice an ambiguity in what I've just assented to. When we say that a certain response to a religious proposition – a religious or irreligious response – is rational, we may be thinking of that response at the level of *token* or *type*. A response token is the response of a particular individual at a particular time and place; a response type is a *way* of responding that can exist purely in the abstract, without ever being 'tokened.' (Of course most relevant response types – including those involving some cognitive state other than belief – will have, corresponding to them, individual persons or groups in the world who *do* respond or have responded in that way.)

Most epistemologists of religion, as suggested earlier, are preoccupied with the evaluation of response *tokens* – though there is unclarity about this and the two levels are sometimes blurred – and for them to raise their sights in the way I am recommending would mean devoting at least as much attention to response types, in (so far as is possible) a clearly distinct and impartial discussion with other inquirers about which response types are rationally *worthy* of being tokened.

There is actually more complexity here than I've indicated so far, since each of the two main levels, concerned with response types and tokens, can be broken down into 'pure' and 'applied' invesigations. When the community of inquiry considers the epistemic worthiness of various types of response to religious propositions, what we want to have enabled is comparative discussion, for anyone who can follow the arguments, about which response to one or another religious proposition the ideal inquirer would or might choose or pursue, carried out by reference to the state of relevant available evidence, the likely (direct or indirect) contribution of a response to epistemic goals, and so on, and perhaps relativized to our early location in the possible history of inquiry. And so we need proposals in search of consensus about general principles by which to proceed here, and also about the results of applying them. At this level the philosopher acts as a sort of 'scout,' exploring the metaphysical and epistemic terrain and rendering a verdict by which others can be guided. She is certainly not putting forward her own beliefs and trying to justify them!

Similarly, we need work both on standards and on their application in connection with the evaluation of response *tokens*. Here we are enabling an assessment of how well people actually do when choosing or pursuing a response in this or that context with whatever (perhaps limited) information they possess. The discussion may involve reference to comparative evaluations but not at the level or in the way previously mentioned; rather it will be relativized to the particular circumstances of the individuals and groups involved – to whether, say, the relevant token responses emerged from a process in which all epistemic duties were fulfilled or intellectual virtues were appropriately cultivated or in which reliability of belief formation was achieved. Of course, as results from the first level, concerned with response types, become better known, we may expect connections between the two levels to manifest themselves more often, since (for example) it will be harder to fulfill epistemic duties without having appropriately taken account of those results.

At both levels we should seek community-wide consensus – where the relevant community is *not* a Christian or Jewish or Islamic community but rather the community of epistemological inquiry. (Otherwise we will have little of the protection from shallow and biased results that we should be especially eager to secure at an early stage of inquiry.) And *both* levels are indeed needed. It would be a great improvement of religious epistemology if we had them.

To see why this must be the case, from an epistemological perspective, simply *compare* what I've just described when indicating the full complexity of the work required at the two levels (and the potential interconnections among results) with an alternative one can find today in this connection, where you have religiously or naturalistically convinced philosophers focused on arguing that they – and members of their partisan communities – can rationally get away with believing as they do, or that their own partisan community's standards are satisfied by their own beliefs. In which of these two ways – the rich multi-leveled discussion aimed at wide community consensus or the alternative – are we most likely, at an early stage of inquiry, to make progress toward the truth on profound matters? And, recognizing that even today not all our results are as egregious as those I've here described in connection with the faulty alternative, how best can we *build on* our best work and minimize the likelihood of epistemological work that will not stand the test of time plus further maturing, intellectually and spiritually? It seems evident that the value of a rich multi-level picture of religious epistemology of the sort I have sketched is confirmed by reflection on these questions. Furthermore, working toward the improvement *it* represents will, in obvious ways, make easier and more natural the *other* two improvements I have discussed in this paper.

4. Conclusion

That these three improvements are needed in religious epistemology, I have at various points suggested, is in some way related to confessional or partisan motives driving much present activity in the field. These are rendered understandable by placing them in a larger context. (Of course 'understandable' is to be distinguished from 'justified.') Seeing how the field has come to have its narrow shape, we can make a conscious decision to no longer let our history or our culture lead us around by the nose, and deliberately improve what we are doing.

Science, as everyone knows, has enormous cachet in western culture today. Ever so many dark corners of human life have been illuminated by it. Almost everyone is inclined to accept that there is scientific knowledge, and that more of it is coming down the pike virtually every day. And contemporary philosophers work hard to accommodate scientific knowledge in their work. Psychologically, the move from awareness of these facts to the idea that science, fully developed, would be capable of telling the *whole* story of reality can be seductive.

History adds to its seductiveness, and also to the apparent force of the idea that theism is all that stands in the way of science being rightly accorded such a glorified status. It was their belief in the existence of a *personal God* that led many early scientists, such as Newton, to assume that the 'whole story' had extra-scientific elements. At many points, as in the struggles precipitated by Darwin's work, scientific explanations have been forged to defeat the previously regnant theistic accounts. Although there are still pockets of resistance, one can detect, over time, a steady weakening of theistic religion's intellectual power in the domain of nature, to the point where no Newton today would give to theism the sort of explanatory role Isaac Newton gave to it in the seventeenth century. But because of the cultural 'constant conjunction' of theism and science over the centuries, a Newton today, especially if as innocent of religious studies as many philosophers appear to be, might still quite naturally behave as though the only alternative to scientific accounts of the whole of reality is given in the name of the theist's God.

Theists in philosophy are, of course, as subject to such cultural and historical influences as anyone else. Turning to the recent history of philosophy, it's interesting to note that over the past few decades we've had some pushback from them to the idea that theism's intellectual power is waning. And where in philosophy has this been most conspicuously present? In religious epistemology! In this context, with the discussion thus shaped, one has to expect an emphasis on the *beliefs* of certain unjustly characterized individuals and groups, and on their defense. Philosophers such as Swinburne and Plantinga, though not denying that theism should stay out of science's way, have also argued (respectively) that there are places theism can go explanatorily which science cannot reach, and that there are experiences which can justifiedly ground theistic belief even if science at some level and to some extent explains them. In making their arguments, they have time and again had to answer objections from scientific naturalists, who hold that theism's explanations are unnecessary or inadequate and that science's explanatory power, when it comes to religious experience, is much more of a threat than theists realize.

But why have philosophers stuck to theism instead of exploring other religious options, or even clearly noting that they exist? In addition to the cultural factors already mentioned, we need to take account of how philosophers such as Plantinga and Swinburne have seen themselves as *giving contemporary Christian theology a hand*: at least to some considerable extent theirs has been *religious* intellectual activity undertaken on behalf of the larger Christian community. The similar dispositions of so many of their acolytes within contemporary religious epistemology, and the activities of those representing a very recent movement explicitly known as analytic theology, lend support to this interpretation. Theistic philosophers doing religious epistemology have not made room for other religious options in part because they are *religiously committed to not doing so*.

At the same time, it's hard not to see scientifically inclined philosophers – and virtually all non-theistic philosophers are scientifically inclined – as seeking to *give contemporary science a hand* by means of their defenses of scientific naturalism. This is perhaps not as obvious as the counterpart disposition among Christians. But it is not implausible to see what is starkly evident in the work of philosophically unsubtle thinkers such as Richard Dawkins or philosophically unmotivated thinkers such as Daniel Dennett as bringing out more clearly a trend of thought that is much more widely influential. In short: there is evidence that religious and scientific *commitment* are in this region of contemporary intellectual life constraining philosophical *imagination*.

By some such route as I have here briefly described, we have arrived at our present situation in religious epistemology. Our field's presently narrow shape, I've said, is thereby made understandable. But the next generation needs to change that shape and make improvements, including such as I have mentioned, if religious epistemology is to become a fully *rational* and *philosophical* activity. In no way is it appropriate for religious epistemology as an investigative enterprise to casually rule out or ignore options which would make both scientific naturalism and theism false, or restrict its efforts to the evaluation of belief tokens when our collaborative responsibilities in relation to various types of response to religious propositions beckon so obviously. This doesn't mean that we must from now on exclude from religious epistemology theists or naturalists bearing arguments in favour of theistic or naturalistic beliefs. Rather, we should distinguish between parochial and *investigative* theism, and between parochial and *investigative* naturalism. Only what is captured by the 'investigative' characterization could, in either case, have a place in philosophy. And those who satisfy it will, I suspect, not find it difficult to see that the three changes I have recommended would indeed

J. L. Schellenberg

make for improvements, or to summon the motivation required to work for their implementation.

Department of Philosophy, Mount Saint Vincent University
john.schellenberg@msvu.ca

Religious Disagreement and Epistemic Intuitions

MICHAEL BERGMANN

Abstract
Religious disagreement is, quite understandably, viewed as a problem for religious belief. In this paper, I consider why religious disagreement is a problem—why it is a potential defeater for religious belief—and I propose a way of dealing with this sort of potential defeater. I begin by focusing elsewhere—on arguments for radical skepticism. In section 1, I consider skeptical arguments proposed as potential defeaters for all of our perceptual and memory beliefs and explain what I think the rational response is to such potential defeaters, emphasizing the way epistemic intuitions are involved in both the skeptical arguments and my recommended response. In section 2, I discuss the way in which peer disagreement—on any topic—is a potential defeater for our beliefs, highlighting the conditions under which recognized disagreement is a successful defeater and those under which it isn't. In the third section, I consider how to use a section-1 type of response to deal with a section-2 type of defeater for religious belief.

Religious disagreement is, quite understandably, viewed as a problem for religious belief. In this paper, I want to consider *why* religious disagreement is a problem—why it is a *potential defeater* for religious belief—and to propose a way of dealing with this sort of potential defeater.

I'll begin by focusing elsewhere—on arguments for radical skepticism. In section 1, I'll consider skeptical arguments proposed as potential defeaters for all of our perceptual and memory beliefs and explain what I think the rational response is to such potential defeaters, emphasizing the way epistemic intuitions are involved in both the skeptical arguments and my recommended response. In section 2, I'll discuss the way in which peer disagreement—on any topic— is a potential defeater for our beliefs, highlighting the conditions under which recognized disagreement is a successful defeater and those under which it isn't. In the third section, I'll consider how to use a section-1 type of response to deal with a section-2 type of defeater for religious belief.

doi:10.1017/S1358246117000224
Royal Institute of Philosophy Supplement **81** 2017

Michael Bergmann

1. Skepticism, Defeaters, and Epistemic Intuitions

1.1 Proposed Defeaters for Perceptual and Memory Beliefs

Skeptical objections are potential defeaters. Arguments for skepticism concerning our perceptual beliefs about the external world are of this sort. I will focus not on rebutting objections, which argue that our perceptual beliefs are false, but on undercutting ones, which argue that our perceptual beliefs aren't formed in a trustworthy way or that we have good reason to doubt that they are formed in a sufficiently trustworthy way. Consider the underdetermination objection to our perceptual beliefs. It begins by noting that these beliefs are not based on arguments or inferences. Instead, they are noninferential beliefs based on sensory experiences that don't guarantee the truth of these beliefs. It seems that we could have these sensory experiences *whether or not* there is an external physical world and *whether or not* the external world is the way these experiences incline us to think that world is. If our perceptual evidence could be the same whether or not the external world is as we are inclined to think it is (on the basis of that evidence), then that evidence *underdetermines* the truth of our perceptual beliefs. One natural response is to seek out arguments—ones that don't rely on our perceptual evidence—for the conclusion that our perceptual evidence makes it probable that our perceptual beliefs are true. There are good reasons for thinking that such arguments aren't available. I won't rehearse those reasons here.[1]

Exactly parallel worries plague our memory beliefs, which are noninferential beliefs based on memory impressions or seemings. These memory seemings don't guarantee the truth of those beliefs: we could have the same memory seemings on which we base our memory beliefs *whether or not* there was a past and *whether or not* the past was the way this memory evidence inclines us to think it was. Our memory evidence, therefore, underdetermines the truth of our memory beliefs, and we don't have any good arguments (that don't rely on memory evidence) for thinking that our memory evidence makes it probable that our memory beliefs are true.[2]

---

[1] But see William Alston, *The Reliability of Sense Perception* (Ithaca: Cornell University Press, 1993) and Richard Fumerton, *Metaepistemology and Skepticism* (Lanham, MD: Rowman and Littlefield, 1995) for helpful discussion.

[2] *Ibid.*

These underdetermination objections to our noninferential perceptual and memory beliefs are potential undercutting defeaters for those beliefs. The question, thus, arises: How can these perceptual and memory beliefs avoid being defeated, given that no good arguments are available for defending those beliefs inferentially against these underdetermination objections?

1.2 Responding to Proposed Defeaters for Perceptual and Memory Beliefs

In my view, the best response to this sort of skeptical worry about perception and memory is a two-step Reidian response that both relies on and responds to epistemic intuitions. The first step in this response is to highlight the strong epistemic intuitions we have that contradict the skeptical conclusions in question. I develop this first step using the work of Thomas Reid and a more recent philosopher, William Tolhurst. The second step is to point out that both the skeptical objections and the Reidian response rely on epistemic intuitions, but the epistemic intuitions on which the skeptical objections rely are much weaker than and, for that reason, outweighed by the stronger epistemic intuitions employed in the Reidian response to the skeptical objection.

Let's start by considering what Reid says on the topic. He notes that it is a first principle that our faculties are reliable and that first principles are properly believed *noninferentially*.[3] Just as we have noninferential beliefs about our immediate physical environment by means of sense perception and about our past by means of memory, so also we have a faculty of common sense by means of which we form noninferential beliefs in first principles.[4] How exactly does this faculty of common sense produce beliefs in first principles? According to Reid:

> We may observe, that opinions which contradict first principles are distinguished from other errors by this; that they are not only false, but absurd: and, to discountenance absurdity, nature has given us a particular emotion, to wit, that of ridicule, which seems intended for this very purpose of putting out of countenance what is absurd, either in opinion or practice.[5]

---

[3]   Thomas Reid, *Essays on the Intellectual Powers of Man*, ed. Derek Brookes (Edinburgh: Edinburgh University Press, 2002 [1785]): 452 & 480.
[4]   *Ibid*. 433.
[5]   *Ibid*. 462.

Michael Bergmann

The suggestion is that when you entertain the contrary of a first principle (e.g., the principle that your faculties are reliable) you experience the emotion of ridicule, which involves the contrary of that first principle seeming absurd. On the basis of this seeming you dismiss as absurd the contrary of the first principle and believe the first principle itself. Thus, noninferential common sense belief in the reliability of your faculties is like noninferential perceptual belief in that both are based on *experiential* evidence—a claim's seeming absurd in the former case and sensory experience in the latter case.[6]

Similar points have been developed in a different context by William Tolhurst who tries to capture the essence of seemings as follows:

> The real difference between seemings and other states that can incline one to believe their content is that seemings have the feel of truth, the feel of a state whose content reveals how things really are. Their felt givenness typically leads one to experience believing that things are as they seem as an objectively fitting or proper response to that seeming. When I merely think about a cat in my yard, imagine this to be the case, or desire that it be the case, my mental state does not have this feel.[7]

Tolhurst calls this feel of a state whose content reveals how things really are its 'felt veridicality'. It is the distinguishing feature of seemings. He goes on to speak of a higher-order awareness of this felt veridicality:

> Felt veridicality can also ground a felt demand that one form a second order belief about the seeming. In calling the feeling of felt veridicality to mind one reflects on one's experiences and considers how they feel. This generates a second order seeming in which the seeming is itself the object of a seeming. When we become self-consciously aware of a seeming it seems to us that

---

[6] For more on this view of Reid's, see Michael Bergmann, *Justification without Awareness* (New York: Oxford University Press, 2006): 206–11. Contrary to what I say there, I now think that the experiential basis of commonsense beliefs is a certain claim's seeming absurd—a seeming that is in some way involved in or connected with the emotion of ridicule—not that emotion itself (we have the emotion *because* the claim seems absurd).

[7] William Tolhurst, 'Seemings', *American Philosophical Quarterly* 35 (1998), 293–302.

the seeming is veridical. This second order seeming is grounded in our awareness of the feel of veridicality.[8]

So, according to Reid, when a normal person considers the suggestion that all her beliefs formed on the basis of her strong perceptual and memory seemings are unreliably formed, it will first *seem* absurd to her that they are unreliably formed and it will then *seem* that they are reliably formed and she'll believe that. (Or at least this is what I take Reid to be suggesting. What follows in the remainder of this section is one way of developing these ideas. Whether this development captures what Reid says in his own writings is not of primary concern to me.) Tolhurst says something similar: when we consider, for example, a memory seeming that p, we become aware of its felt veridicality and this makes it seem to us that the memory seeming that p is veridical; on the basis of this higher-order seeming, we believe that the memory belief that p, based on that memory seeming that p, is formed in a reliable and nonmisleading way, contrary to the skeptical scenario that, according to the objector, should make us have doubts.

These higher-order seemings that our first-order beliefs are reliably formed or that our first-order seemings are veridical are examples of epistemic intuitions. Epistemic intuitions are like moral intuitions, which are seemings about moral matters, the difference being that epistemic intuitions are seemings about epistemic matters. Both are normative seemings. Just as one can have moral intuitions about particular cases, mid-level principles, or higher-level principles, so also one can have epistemic intuitions about particular cases, mid-level principles, or higher-level principles. The Reidian response to the underdetermination objection to our perceptual and memory beliefs relies on epistemic intuitions. The skeptical objection raises doubts about the reliability of our noninferential perceptual and memory beliefs or about the veridicality of our sensory experience or our perceptual or memory seemings. The Reidian reply is to reject those doubts and affirm the reliability of those beliefs and the veridicality of the seemings on which they're based. In doing this, the one endorsing the Reidian reply is forming a higher-level belief about the trustworthiness of our faculties and this higher-level belief is based on epistemic intuitions. Responses to skepticism in this Reidian or commonsensist vein have been championed by

---

[8] *Ibid.* 299. For further discussions of what seemings are see Michael Bergmann, 'Externalist Justification and the Role of Seemings', *Philosophical Studies* 166 (2013), 163–84.

Michael Bergmann

many since the time of Reid, including G.E. Moore and Chisholm, but also contemporary epistemologists such as Jim Pryor and John Greco.[9]

(I should note here that not all who support a Reidian response to skepticism would focus on seemings or evidence in the form of epistemic intuitions (Greco, for example, wouldn't). I happen to think such a focus is a natural and plausible Reidian way to account for what in fact happens when we humans hear about and then rationally dismiss radical skeptical hypotheses and objections. However, it is not my view that having such seemings or intuitions is the only way any possible cognizer could rationally respond to skeptical objections. Nor is it my view that beliefs can't be justified unless they're based on seemings of some kind (e.g., memorial, perceptual, intuitional, etc.). It's just that I think rational *human* beliefs very often *happen to be* based, at least in part, on seemings of some kind.[10])

Chisholm famously cites the Reidian response to Humean skeptical worries as a paradigm instance of a view he called 'particularism'.[11] The Humean skeptic believes an epistemic principle saying that we can't know anything about the external world or the past unless we have strong arguments for our conclusions—arguments beginning with premises about our current experience. Reid recognized that such a principle implies that we don't have any knowledge about the external world or the past, since no strong arguments of that kind are available. But he thought it was clear that we *do* have knowledge of the existence of the external world and the past. As a result, Reid and Moore and others in this tradition reject the epistemic principle on which the Humean skeptical argument depends. This is called a '*particularist*' response to Humean skepticism because it gives more weight to intuitions about the epistemic status of particular beliefs than to intuitions concerning general epistemic principles about what is required for justification or knowledge—principles of the sort employed in skeptical objections.

[9] See John Greco, *Putting Skeptics In Their Place* (New York: Cambridge University Press, 2000) and James Pryor, 'The Skeptic and the Dogmatist', *Noûs* 34 (2000), 517–49.
[10] See Bergmann 2013 *op. cit.* where I defend externalism and reject Phenomenal Conservatism, despite my friendliness to talk of seemings.
[11] See Roderick Chisholm, 'The Problem of the Criterion', *The Foundations of Knowing* (Minneapolis: University of Minnesota Press, 1982), 68–9. Particularism as Chisholm understands it should not be confused with moral particularism of the sort defended by Jonathan Dancy, *Ethics without Principles*, (Oxford: Oxford University Press, 2004).

An important thing to notice is that, in making this response, the Reidian particularist is doing the same sort of thing that the skeptic is doing. After all, how does the skeptic know that her epistemic principles are true? Presumably the epistemic principles, on which the skeptic relies in proposing her skeptical objections, are believed on the basis of epistemic intuitions. (Indeed, just as it's hard to see how moral beliefs are in fact justified without relying in *some* way at *some* point on moral intuitions, it's also difficult to see how skeptical arguments—for epistemic conclusions about what we epistemically shouldn't believe—are in fact justified without relying in *some* way at *some* point on epistemic intuitions.[12]) The Reidian can concede that there may be some initial appeal to the epistemic intuitions on which skeptical objections rely. But she goes on to insist that the strength of these skepticism-inducing epistemic intuitions pales in comparison to the strength of the epistemic intuitions in support of the rationality of beliefs about particular cases and in support of the reliability of the belief-forming faculties that produced them.

Putting all this in terms of defeaters, what we have is the following. I form my noninferentially justified perceptual and memory beliefs. I then become aware of the underdetermination objection—a skeptical objection suggesting that I should be doubtful of the reliability of these perceptual and memory beliefs. This is a proposed defeater for these beliefs and it is based, at least in part, on epistemic intuitions (e.g., the intuition that I should withhold judgment about the reliability of my beliefs based on evidence that doesn't guarantee their truth—at least until I've got an argument that those beliefs are made probable by that evidence). But when I consider the higher-level claim that my perceptual and memory beliefs aren't formed in a trustworthy way, I have the strong higher-level seeming that this is false and that, in fact, my perceptual and memory beliefs *are* formed in a trustworthy way. On the basis of this epistemic intuition, I deny the claim that they're unreliably formed and I also deny the skeptic's premise, which says that, in light of the underdetermination

---

[12]   There is more to be said about this than I can get into here. For an initial statement, without endorsement, of some aspects of this line of thought in connection with *moral* beliefs, see Walter Sinnott-Armstrong, *Moral Skepticisms* (New York: Oxford University Press, 2006), 74–77. Similar points can be made in connection with beliefs about epistemic matters. In the abstract, there are the possibilities of basing beliefs about epistemic value on authoritative testimony or on some 'inference to the best explanation' arguments for realism about epistemic value and for the reliability of our beliefs about epistemic matters. But in fact, such beliefs are, I think, typically noninferentially based on epistemic intuition.

objection, I epistemically *should* be doubtful about or withhold my perceptual and memory beliefs. In short, this proposed defeater is deflected[13] by my reliance on epistemic intuitions, ones that are stronger than the epistemic intuitions supporting the defeater. As a result, my justified perceptual and memory beliefs avoid being defeated by this skeptical objection.

Moreover, although epistemologists can explain in some detail how this happens (by mentioning the sorts of things I've said above and by developing those remarks at length), this Reidian response works just as well for the philosophically naïve. For example, an ordinary person might watch the movie *The Matrix* for the first time and, as she walks out of the theater, she might consider the possibility that her own perceptual beliefs are massively unreliable and she might wonder how she could rule out this possibility. She might even wonder if it is sensible for her to continue trusting her sensory experience. But soon after she considers this worry, she dismisses it as implausible and affirms that it would be silly to be skeptical in that way, on the basis of such concerns, about her perception. This ordinary person is responding to the underdetermination objection in basically the same way that Reid is, despite the fact that she wouldn't describe her response in the way I've been describing the Reidian response.

1.3 Satisfying the Skeptic

Notice that the claim here is *not* that this sort of response will satisfy the skeptical objector by offering her what she'll consider to be a successful proof that the objection fails. The claim, rather, is that these perceptual and memory beliefs can remain rational, in the way noted, in the face of these potential defeaters. This is because even if the skeptical objector is not satisfied by these responses, it's simply false that, in such a situation, rationality requires me to give up those perceptual and memory beliefs.[14] And what matters for

---

[13] Deflecting a defeater is to be distinguished from defeating a defeater. Defeating a defeater (on one natural construal) causes that defeater to lose its defeating power. Deflecting a defeater is different: it prevents a potential defeater from having any defeating power to begin with.

[14] It might seem true *to the skeptic* that, in such a situation, rationality requires me to give up those perceptual and memory beliefs. But that's because the skeptic doesn't have veridical epistemic intuitions (more on this in the next subsection).

epistemic defeat is not what the skeptic finds satisfying but what rationality in fact requires.

Given that this reply won't satisfy the skeptic, how is this a helpful response to skeptical objections? It can be helpful in a couple of ways. First, it's helpful for people who share the epistemic intuitions most non-skeptics share but who aren't sure how best to respond to skeptical objections, which seem to carry some weight. This response helps these non-skeptics to see that although there is a tempting appeal to the skeptic's epistemic intuitions, they are ultimately non-veridical and overridden by considerably stronger epistemic intuitions to the contrary. Second, it's also helpful for skeptical objectors for two reasons: (i) It helps objectors to see (if they haven't already) that those to whom they're objecting have an internally coherent response that fits their non-skeptical epistemic intuitions, which shows that the situation for the non-skeptic isn't as problematic as skeptical objectors sometimes think. (ii) It helps objectors to come face to face (if they haven't already) with the charge that although the epistemic intuitions supporting their objection are understood and to some degree appreciated by non-skeptics, these skeptical intuitions are viewed with skepticism by non-skeptics as non-veridical epistemic illusions; being faced with this charge might go some way toward helping these objectors to see that their skeptical objections aren't as strong as they may have supposed.

1.4 Internal Rationality, External Rationality, and the Unconvinced Skeptic

I've said that our perceptual and memory beliefs remain rational and justified in the face of the skeptic's underdetermination objection. For the most part, I've been using the terms 'rationality' and 'justification' as synonyms referring to what we might call 'internal rationality'. Internal rationality differs from external rationality as follows: a belief is internally rational if the belief formation process is going as it epistemically should downstream from experience (i.e., in response to the subject's conscious mental states, which constitute her evidence); a belief is externally rational if the belief formation process is going as it epistemically should both upstream and downstream from the experience.[15] For example, a perceptual belief is internally rational if it is an epistemically appropriate response to the subject's

---

[15]   This distinction is introduced by Alvin Plantinga in his *Warranted Christian Belief* (New York: Oxford University Press, 2000), 110–12.

conscious mental states, in particular her sensory experiences. But a perceptual belief can be internally rational even if these sensory experiences were not produced in an epistemically appropriate way but were, instead, artificially produced by a deceptive demon or a computer, as in the movie *The Matrix*. In that case, the perceptual belief based on these artificially produced sensory experiences would be internally rational but not externally rational.

(Notice that one can be either an internalist or an externalist about internal rationality. For example, if you think that what makes a belief an epistemically appropriate response to your evidence base is that it is a proper functioning response to it or a reliable response to it, then you are an externalist about internal rationality. But if you think that what makes a belief an epistemically appropriate response to your evidence base is that your belief *fits* that evidence base, where this fittingness relation holds of necessity between that belief and that particular evidence base, in virtue of some of the intrinsic consciously accessible features of the relata, then you are, presumably, an evidentialist and an internalist about internal rationality. My own view is that externalism is true. So although I think we humans typically form beliefs on the basis of conscious mental states, I also think (i) that it's possible for beliefs to be justified even if they aren't based on conscious mental states and (ii) that justification supervenes not on our mental states but on facts about what proper function requires.[16])

With the distinction between internal and external rationality in mind, consider what I've said about satisfying the skeptic. I've said that epistemic intuitions in support of the justification of our perceptual and memory beliefs are much stronger than and outweigh the epistemic intuitions in support of the premises used in the underdetermination objection. But what if the skeptic's epistemic intuitions are different? What if her epistemic intuitions in support of the premises used in the underdetermination objection are as strong as or stronger than those indicating that her perceptual and memory beliefs are justified and reliably formed? Perhaps in that case, it won't be *internally* rational for the skeptic to join the Reidian respondent in treating the epistemic intuitions in support of the underdetermination objection as illusory; and perhaps that means that the skeptic can't save the internal rationality of her perceptual and memory beliefs in the Reidian way I suggest above. So perhaps the skeptic is internally rational to endorse the

---

[16] For further discussion see Bergmann 2006 *op. cit.* and Bergmann 2013 *op. cit.*

underdetermination objection on the basis of her epistemic intuitions, even though the non-skeptic is internally rational to endorse the Reidian response on the basis of *her* epistemic intuitions. What's internally rational can differ between people if their evidence (in this case, the epistemic intuitions they have) differs.

I've also said, in the previous subsection, that what rationality in fact requires is *not* that we give up our perceptual and memory beliefs in response to the underdetermination objection. The point here is that having epistemic intuitions in support of the underdetermination objection that are as strong as or stronger than those in support of the justification of our perceptual and memory beliefs is *not* in accord with *external* rationality. So even if the skeptic is internally rational in (i) endorsing the underdetermination objection on the basis of her epistemic intuitions that support it and (ii) withholding (or holding less firmly) her perceptual and memory beliefs in the face of that objection, she is not *externally* rational in doing so. The externally rational thing for the skeptic to do is to have weaker epistemic intuitions in support of the underdetermination objection and to have them outweighed by much stronger epistemic intuitions in support of the justification of her perceptual and memory beliefs, leading her to treat the skeptical intuitions as illusory. External rationality will result in this person continuing firmly to hold her perceptual and memory beliefs, despite the skeptical objection.

What is my basis for this view about what external rationality requires? Reliance on epistemic intuitions. Of course, the skeptic won't view things this way, so she will think she is being misjudged as irrational by the non-skeptic. (I've conversed with perceptual skeptics who feel this way.) But a similar point holds in the other direction: the non-skeptic won't view things the way the skeptic does, so she will think she is being misjudged as irrational by the skeptic. It's not easy to see a way forward that will guarantee a resolution between these two perspectives, a way for the skeptic and non-skeptic to engage in a philosophical conversation that is likely to bring about a shared point of view on the matter.

1.5 Concerns about Epistemic Circularity

Various objections can be raised against reliance on epistemic intuition. One kind of objection is based on work in experimental philosophy that raises concerns about the reliability of epistemic intuition. Unfortunately, I don't have the space to enter into a discussion of this challenge in this paper.[17] Another sort of objection to reliance on epistemic intuition asks the following question: What happens if the skeptic takes the underdetermination objection and uses it against beliefs formed on the basis of epistemic intuitions? (After all, these epistemic intuitions don't guarantee the truth of the beliefs based on them.) Won't there be trouble if one tries to use the Reidian response to defend epistemic intuitions against this objection? I.e., won't it be viciously circular to respond to the skeptic about epistemic intuitions by relying on epistemic intuitions to confirm the trustworthiness and rationality of relying on epistemic intuitions?

Before addressing that concern, let's consider a related worry that this skeptic about epistemic intuition faces—the worry that using the underdetermination objection to support skepticism about epistemic intuitions is self-undermining. This objection itself relies on premises that are based, ultimately, on epistemic intuitions (e.g., the intuition that I epistemically should withhold judgment about the reliability of my beliefs based on evidence that doesn't guarantee their truth—at least until I've got an argument that those beliefs are made probable by that evidence). So the skeptic appears to be guilty of relying on epistemic intuitions to argue that we can't trust epistemic intuitions. The skeptic might respond by pointing out that it's possible to learn that a belief source is problematic by discovering that it indicates its own unreliability.[18] That is a response worth taking seriously. But the question is whether, in making such a discovery, the belief source should be mistrusted wholesale or whether, instead, our mistrust should be directed more narrowly at

---

[17]   But, for some supportive presentations of this kind of objection, see Jonathan Weinberg et al., 'Normativity and Epistemic Intuitions', *Philosophical Topics* 29 (2001), 429–60 and Joshua Alexander et al., 'The "Unreliability" of Epistemic Intuitions', *Current Controversies in Experimental Philosophy*, eds. Edouard Machery and Elizabeth O'Neill (New York: Routledge, 2014), 128–45. For some replies to these kinds of objections, see John Bengson, 'Experimental Attacks on Intuitions and Answers', *Philosophy and Phenomenological Research* 86 (2013), 495–532; Jennifer Nagel, 'Epistemic intuitions', *Philosophy Compass* 2 (2007), 792–819; Jennifer Nagel, 'Intuitions and Experiments: A defense of the case method', *Philosophy and Phenomenological Research* 85 (2012), 495–527; and Kenneth Boyd and Jennifer Nagel, 'The Reliability of Epistemic Intuitions', *Current Controversies in Experimental Philosophy*, eds. Edouard Machery and Elizabeth O'Neill (New York: Routledge, 2014), 109–27.

[18]   For a nice example of this see Fumerton *op. cit.* 50–51.

the alleged indicators of the source's supposed untrustworthiness. The Reidian will be happy to acknowledge that our belief sources are imperfect. But in this particular case, she'll be inclined to think that the problem is with the epistemic intuitions behind the underdetermination objection, not with epistemic intuition as a whole.

Let's return, briefly, to the circularity problem that afflicts the Reidian anti-skeptic who relies on epistemic intuitions in forming the belief that her epistemic intuitions are veridical. Is that a problematic kind of epistemic circularity? The short answer is that relying on epistemic intuitions in forming the belief that one's epistemic intuitions are veridical needn't be problematic even though it does manifest a kind of epistemic circularity. (A belief, B, is epistemically circular if (i) it is a belief in the trustworthiness of a belief source S and (ii) the person holding B depends on belief source S in forming or holding B.) Sometimes epistemic circularity is benign. In the case of epistemic intuition, it is benign when the person with such intuitions neither is nor (epistemically) should be seriously questioning or doubting the trustworthiness or veridicality of these intuitions. I don't have the space here to give a detailed account of this way of defending benign epistemic circularity, but I do so elsewhere.[19]

2. Disagreement as a Potential Defeater

As a general rule, disagreement about p provides a defeater for your belief that p when you think the person disagreeing with you is your *epistemic peer* (or better) with respect to p, which is to say you think that (a) that person's evidence with respect to p is approximately as good, epistemically, as yours (or better) and that (b) when it comes to belief-formation with respect to p, that person is approximately as good, epistemically, as you are (or better) at responding to such evidence.[20] The problem generated by peer disagreement is that if you think the other person's evidence with respect to p is as good as yours and that the person responds to such evidence as well as you do, then (assuming it's initially rational to trust yourself on this matter) you have good reason to think that each of you (in forming beliefs about whether or not p) forms them in a reliable and

---

[19] See Bergmann 2006 *op. cit.* 179–211.

[20] See Michael Bergmann, 'Religious Disagreement and Rational Demotion', *Oxford Studies in Philosophy of Religion,* ed. Jonathan Kvanvig (New York: Oxford University Press, 2015), n. 2 for further discussion.

Michael Bergmann

nonmisleading way. But if you then come to realize that the two of you disagree about p (one thinking it's true, the other thinking it's false), you have good reason to think that either that person's belief or your belief with respect to p is formed in a misleading way. At this point, you have two main options: either (i) you can give up believing (by withholding or disbelieving) that your belief that p is formed in a reliable and nonmisleading way; or (ii) you can give up believing that the other person is your epistemic peer, in effect demoting that person from epistemic peer to epistemic inferior, at least with respect to p on this particular occasion. (Demotion of this sort can take place in two ways. I might demote you from being an epistemic peer with respect to p to being an epistemic inferior with respect to p, thinking that you have worse evidence than I do or that you aren't as good as I am at responding to such evidence. Or I might demote you from 'believing like an epistemic peer with respect to p on this occasion' to 'believing like an epistemic inferior with respect to p on this occasion'. If I demote you in the first way, I'm demoting you from peer to inferior; if I demote you in the second way, I'm demoting your believing on a particular occasion from peer-like believing to inferior-like believing. To simplify the discussion, I will refer to both as demotion from peer to inferior. What really matters, in connection with demotion and defeat in cases of disagreement, is the second kind of demotion.[21]) If you do or epistemically should take option (i), you have a defeater for your belief that p.[22] If you take option (ii) and you do so rationally, then your recognition that the other person disagrees with you no longer threatens to defeat your belief that p.

We can formulate these ideas in a principle as follows:

> D: If in response to recognizing that S disagrees with you about p (which you heretofore rationally believed), you either do or epistemically should disbelieve or seriously question or doubt the claim that you are, on this occasion, both trustworthy with respect to p and *more* trustworthy than S with respect to p, then your belief that p is defeated by this recognition; otherwise not.

This account of disagreement-based defeaters gives rise to the following question: when can I rationally demote (or continue to view as an

---

[21] See *ibid*. 26 for further discussion.
[22] This implies that unjustified beliefs can defeat justified ones. See Bergmann 2006 *op. cit.* 163–8 for some discussion of this.

epistemic inferior[23]) someone who disagrees with me? The answer, I think, depends on at least three kinds of evidence:

p-evidence: evidence bearing on p, the disputed claim;

Rp-evidence: evidence bearing on Rp, the proposition that your belief that p is formed in a reliable and nonmisleading way;

R~p-evidence: evidence bearing on R~p, the proposition that your assumed peer's belief that ~p is formed in a reliable and nonmisleading way.

Although it is difficult to say exactly where to draw the line between cases of defeat and cases where you can rationally demote the one disagreeing with you, we can say this much: When your p-evidence and Rp-evidence are strongly supportive (of p and Rp, respectively) and your R~p-evidence is no more than weakly supportive (of R~p), it is rational to demote the one disagreeing with you. But when your R~p-evidence is at least as strongly supportive as your Rp-evidence and your p-evidence, then it is not rational to demote and you have a defeater.[24]

Consider three examples that illustrate these points:

Restaurant Case: You and three friends are sharing a meal and decide to split the check evenly. In your head, you calculate a 20% tip and divide by four and, rounding up, come up with $47 each. You believe this is correct because you did it carefully. But then your friend at the table does the same thing and tells you she came up with $43 each.[25]

The standard reaction to this case is that this sort of disagreement gives you a defeater. A natural way to explain this assessment is to point out that your R~p-evidence (concerning whether your friend can do this sort of calculation well) is about as strongly supportive as your Rp-evidence (concerning whether you can do it well) and your p-evidence (concerning what each share of the bill should be).

---

23   For convenience, I'll refer to cases where a person is viewed as an epistemic inferior without first being viewed as an epistemic peer or better as cases of demoting, even if strictly speaking, there is no demotion in such a case from a peer or better to an inferior.

24   Thanks to Nichole Smith and Joel Ballivian for pressing me to clarify the ideas in this paragraph.

25   This is an oft-discussed case in the literature on disagreement. See David Christensen, 'Epistemology of Disagreement: The Good News', *Philosophical Review* 116 (2007), 187–217 for an early discussion of it.

As a result, you can't rationally demote your friend with respect to the proposition over which you disagree, which leaves you with a defeater.

Consider next two other examples:

Math Conference Case: Suppose you are a fifty-year-old full professor of mathematics, well-informed in your field. You are at a mathematics conference and, in the conference hotel, you see a man your age dressed in the way a typical math professor attending such a conference would be dressed, reading a sign giving the conference schedule. You ask him if he's here for the conference and he says he is. At this point, you assume he's at least roughly your peer on mathematical questions up to at least the level of, say, first-year university calculus. However, a little later you are having a conversation with him in which he asserts things that demonstrate a level of mathematical incompetence you'd expect from someone whose SAT score in math was so low, he couldn't get into a community college. (Suppose he asserts ten things, each of which is the denial of a mathematical claim so obviously true that any ordinary high school freshman earning a C or higher in math classes would easily see that it's true.) The man persists in his beliefs, even after you tell him that you disagree and can see that his beliefs are obviously mistaken.[26]

Jury Case: The police haul you in, accusing you of stealing my laptop. The evidence against you is strong. There are reliable witnesses claiming to have seen you at my house at the time the crime occurred. You are known to have a motive to do me harm. And the laptop was found on your property. The jury, upon hearing the evidence, is convinced and believes that you are guilty. But you have a clear memory of being on a solitary hike outside of the city at the time, although you have no witnesses who can confirm this. You report this clear memory to the jury, but they aren't impressed.[27]

In each of these cases, the natural response is to think that your belief is not defeated by the disagreement (with the person at the math conference or the jury members). We can easily explain this by pointing out that your R~p-evidence is at best weakly supportive and your p-evidence and your Rp-evidence are strongly supportive.

---

[26] I introduced this case in Bergmann 2015 *op. cit.* 28.
[27] This is a slightly altered version of an example from Plantinga 2000 *op. cit.* 450.

Your R~p-evidence is at best weakly supportive because you don't
have very strong evidence that the person at the math conference is
good at correctly answering those math questions (you just
assumed this upon hearing him say he was attending the conference)
or that the jury members are as good as you are at determining your
whereabouts at the time of the crime (after all, you have clear memories of what you were doing at the time and they don't). Your p-evidence is strongly supportive because of how intuitively obvious the
math answers are and how clear your memories are of your whereabouts at the time of the crime. And your Rp-evidence is also strongly
supportive because it consists of strong epistemic intuitions in
support of the trustworthiness of the relevant memory and mathematical seemings.

3. Is Religious Disagreement a Defeater?

To simplify the discussion of religious disagreement, I'll focus on one
particular religious belief: the belief that God (a perfect person who
created the universe) exists. There is clearly disagreement on this
topic. The question is whether it results in a defeater. The answer
will vary depending in part on how strongly supportive the relevant
bits of evidence are (p-evidence, Rp-evidence, and R~p-evidence).
In what follows, I will explain why I think there are some cases
where disagreement does not provide a defeater for theistic belief.

3.1 p-evidence, Rp-evidence, and R~p-evidence for Theistic Belief

First, let's consider the p-evidence, the evidence concerning theism
itself. I will be ignoring theistic arguments and focusing instead on
evidence on which noninferential theistic belief is based. There are
various kinds of experiential evidence for noninferential theistic
belief. One kind is dramatic religious experience, including in particular perceptual experience of God. In his *Perceiving God*, Alston
focuses on mystical perception, in which God seems to reveal
himself in some vivid or shocking or overwhelming way. Alston
thinks of it as perception because God is (allegedly) perceived as
doing something vis-à-vis the perceiver or as having some perceivable
property such as goodness, power, or kindness.[28] Because this kind of

[28]   William Alston, *Perceiving God* (Ithaca: Cornell University Press,
1991), 14–28.

Michael Bergmann

perceptual experience of God is rare, I will set it aside and focus instead on a different kind of experiential evidence for noninferential theistic belief, namely, theistic seemings.

Just as noninferential memory, moral, and mathematical belief are often based on memory, moral and mathematical seemings, so also, noninferential theistic belief is often based on theistic seemings.[29] Many things can trigger ordinary theistic seemings. They might be triggered by things upstream from experience, including things such as the direct activity of God (this is one way of thinking about at least some instances of what the Christian tradition calls 'the testimony of the Holy Spirit'). But they can also be triggered by things downstream from experience such as feelings of guilt or being forgiven or desperate fear or gratitude; other triggers can be experiences of awe at the grandeur and majesty of oceans, mountains, or sky.[30] Another way theistic seemings can arise is in response to the spoken or written testimony of others: we encounter the testimony and what is said simply seems right.[31] Theistic seemings can also result from ruminating upon what we have learned about the immensity, complexity, mysteriousness, and possible origins of nature and of the human mind.[32] Likewise, a consideration of the apparent design in nature (e.g., in the biological world and in Big Bang cosmology) can prompt a seeming that God designed these things, a seeming that isn't based on any argument from design and that is compatible

[29]   Plantinga seems to have theistic seemings in mind in his 2000 *op. cit.* 182–3 when he discusses the nature of the experiences involved in the operation of the *sensus divinitatus,* which produces belief in God. There he notes that what such experiences have in common is that they all include doxastic experience. And it is clear that what Plantinga thinks of as doxastic experience is the sort of thing that is involved in having a seeming. See Plantinga 2000 *op. cit.* 110–11 and Plantinga, *Warrant and Proper Function* (New York: Oxford University Press, 1993), 190–93.

[30]   Plantinga 2000 *op. cit.* 174.

[31]   As Plantinga writes (*ibid.* 250): 'We read Scripture, or something presenting scriptural teaching, or hear the gospel preached, or are told of it by parents, or encounter a scriptural teaching as the conclusion of an argument (or conceivably even as an object of ridicule), or in some other way encounter a proclamation of the Word. What is said simply seems right; it seems compelling; one finds oneself saying, "Yes, that's right, that's the truth of the matter; this is indeed the word of the Lord".'

[32]   Charles Sanders Peirce, 'A Neglected Argument for the Reality of God', *Collected Papers of Charles Sanders Peirce: Volumes V and VI*, eds. Charles Hartshorne and Paul Weiss (Cambridge, MA: Harvard University, 1965 [1908]), 6.452–85.

with believing in evolution.[33] These theistic seemings aren't the results of simply considering the proposition *God exists* and finding that it seems true; nor are they conclusions of arguments. They are more like what Audi calls 'conclusions of reflection', which are not based on inferences from premises but instead emerge noninferentially from an awareness of a variety of observations, experiences, and considerations over a (perhaps long) period of time.[34] Thus, in a certain sense, the evidence I'm thinking of doesn't consist solely of theistic seemings. It also includes many recent and long past observations, experiences, testimony, considerations, and the traces of these retained in memory out of which these theistic seemings emerge noninferentially upon reflection. It is often the case that we are unable to trace the origins of our theistic seemings. But, as Ernest Sosa and Graham Oppy point out in other contexts, the fact that we can't trace the origins of our seemings doesn't show that the beliefs based on those seemings aren't rational or trustworthy.[35] And just as memory, moral, and mathematical seemings can be weak or very strong, so also theistic seemings can be weak or very strong. The kind of p-evidence that I have in mind consists of *strong* theistic seemings. These theistic seemings might not be as strong as our strongest perceptual and memory seemings. But this doesn't mean they aren't strong enough to be used in making theistic belief rational in the face of disagreement.

The accounts given of what justifies noninferential theistic beliefs so based will be similar to accounts given of the justification of perceptual, memory, mathematical, or moral beliefs. Evidentialists will say that theistic beliefs so based are justified if the beliefs fit the evidence on which they're based.[36] Reliabilists will say that beliefs so based are justified if the processes by which such beliefs are formed

[33]   Alvin Plantinga, *Where the Conflict Really Lies* (New York: Oxford University Press, 2011), 240–264.
[34]   Robert Audi, *The Good in the Right* (Princeton, NJ: Princeton University Press, 2004), 45–6.
[35]   Ernest Sosa, 'The Epistemology of Disagreement', *Social Epistemology,* eds. Adrian Haddock et al. (Oxford University Press, 2010), 278–97 and Graham Oppy, 'Disagreement', *International Journal for Philosophy of Religion* 68 (2010), 183–99.
[36]   Chris Tucker, 'Phenomenal Conservatism and Evidentialism in Religious Epistemology', *Evidence and Religious Belief,* eds. Raymond VanArragon and Kelly James Clark (Oxford: Oxford University Press, 2011), 52–73.

Michael Bergmann

are reliable.[37] Proper functionalists will say that beliefs so based are justified if they are produced by properly functioning cognitive faculties in the appropriate cognitive environment.[38] Insofar as theistic beliefs can be fitting responses to theistic seemings and insofar as theistic beliefs based on theistic seemings can be reliably formed or produced by properly functioning faculties, noninferential theistic beliefs formed on these bases can (according to these familiar accounts of epistemic normativity) be justified or rational.

As I suggested earlier, in order for theistic beliefs based on theistic seemings to be *internally* rational, things must be going as they epistemically should downstream from experience (i.e., they must be epistemically fitting responses to triggers consisting of other current or previous mental states of the subject). Thus, on my view, it often isn't merely strength of seeming that is required, where that strength is understood subjectively. For example, in cases where theistic seemings are conclusions of reflection, then, even though they aren't inferential, they must be epistemically appropriate responses to previous mental states of the subject (if such seemings are to be sources of justified belief). But in cases where the theistic seemings aren't formed in response to previous mental states, what matters for internal rationality is mainly that they aren't failing to be appropriately responsive to any defeating evidence one might have.[39]

The relevant Rp-evidence is the higher-order seeming that the theistic seemings, on the basis of which one believes that God exists, are veridical. It's not that the theist finds it absurd that any seeming on a religious topic could be nonveridical. Rather, when she ponders the particular theistic seemings on which her own theistic beliefs are based, it seems strongly to her (because of an awareness of their felt veridicality) that these theistic seemings are veridical. These higher-order seemings are epistemic intuitions about particular theistic beliefs. They are the very same sort of evidence that makes us think our strong memory, moral, and mathematical seemings are veridical. The kind of Rp-evidence I have in mind, then, is *strong* epistemic intuition in support of the veridicality of the strong theistic seemings on which our theistic beliefs are based. Again, these

---

[37]   Alston 1991 *op. cit.* and William Alston, 'Knowledge of God', *Faith, Reason, and Skepticism*, ed. Marcus Hester (Philadelphia: Temple University Press, 1992), 6–49.

[38]   Plantinga 2000 *op. cit.*

[39]   Thanks to Joel Ballivian and John Greco for pressing me to clarify the points made in this paragraph.

epistemic intuitions in support of our theistic seemings might not be as strong as our strongest epistemic intuitions in support of the veridicality of our perceptual and memory seemings. But this doesn't mean they aren't strong enough to be used in making theistic belief rational in the face of disagreement.

Our overall Rp-evidence is more strongly supportive when it also includes another kind of Rp-evidence, namely, the recognition that many other people are theists, including many who are exceedingly intelligent and aware of potential defeaters for theism, whose moral character is extremely admirable, and who are very mature[40] and practically wise in ways that enable them to flourish in their environments. These considerations have to be balanced against the fact that many non-theists are also like this. But they still make our Rp-evidence more strongly supportive than it would be in the absence of such awareness of numerous other intellectually and morally impressive theists.[41]

The theist's R~p-evidence is her evidence bearing on whether the belief that theism is false, held by those who disagree with her, is formed in a reliable and nonmisleading way. I don't think the theist has very strong evidence that the atheist's belief on this matter is reliable. Of course, educated theists are aware that both atheists and theists have developed arguments *for* their positions and responded to arguments *against* their positions. They are also aware that, just as with other topics in philosophy, there is a lot of variation in the assessments of these arguments and responses. If one considered only the philosophical literature on theistic and atheistic arguments, it would be very controversial indeed to say that it gives us strong evidence that the atheist's beliefs on this matter are reliable (it would be about as controversial as saying that the philosophical literature on incompatibilism about free will gives us strong evidence that the incompatibilist's beliefs about incompatibilism are reliable). Focusing only on atheistic arguments, the strongest seem to be arguments from evil and, although some of those arguments are more plausible than others, it seems fair to say that none of them are knockdown arguments and none of them are strong enough to rationally require consent from all informed intelligent people.[42]

---

[40]   I.e., emotionally secure, focused on others, and adept at respectfully and compassionately negotiating the complexities of human interactions and relationships.

[41]   See Bergmann 2015 *op. cit.* 41–42 for further discussion of this point.

[42]   For some discussion of arguments from evil that lends support to this claim, see Plantinga 2000 *op. cit.* 458–99; William Alston, 'The Inductive

Michael Bergmann

Moreover, even if a theist thinks that theistic arguments aren't strong enough to justify theistic belief and that atheistic arguments have some force, that isn't sufficiently strong evidence for thinking that the atheist's beliefs on this matter are reliable. Consider again the Jury Case. In that example, you've been accused of a crime and you agree that the jury has very strong evidence for thinking you are guilty. Nevertheless, your overall evidence for thinking that the jurors' beliefs about your guilt are reliable is *not* strong. This is because you think their evidence is deficient in an important way in which your own evidence (which includes your vivid memories) is not. Something similar might be true of the theist who is thinking about the atheist who relies on atheistic arguments that have some force. Although the theist might have good reason to think that the most sophisticated atheists are as good as anyone else at formulating valid arguments with somewhat appealing premises on the topic of God's existence, the theist doesn't have good reason to be equally impressed with the atheist's capacity or tendency to have appropriate theistic seemings and to respond properly to them. The theist has her theistic seemings and her higher-order seemings about these theistic seemings, which assure her of their veridicality. But when she considers the atheist, what she notices is that the atheist apparently lacks these seemings, or at least that she has them only weakly and doesn't have or trust any higher-order seemings about the veridicality of her theistic seemings. In noticing these things about the atheist, the theist isn't thereby getting strong evidence that these atheistic beliefs are being formed in reliable and nonmisleading ways. If anything, she's getting evidence to the contrary, given her own theistic seemings and their felt veridicality. The theist's assessment of the atheist who has somewhat forceful atheistic arguments but who lacks or doesn't trust theistic seemings is like your assessment (in the Jury Case) of the jurors who have strong evidence for your guilt but who lack the memories you have of your innocence: you don't have strong evidence for the reliability of the jurors about your guilt and the theist doesn't have strong evidence for the reliability of the atheist about whether God exists. Importantly, evidence for the atheist's overall intelligence, virtue, etc. doesn't count as strong

---

Argument from Evil and the Human Cognitive Condition', *Philosophical Perspectives* 5 (1991): 29–67; and Michael Bergmann, 'Skeptical Theism and the Problem of Evil', *The Oxford Handbook to Philosophical Theology*, eds. Thomas Flint and Michael Rea (New York: Oxford University Press, 2009), 374–99.

evidence for her reliability on the topic of theism, since such intelligence and virtue are compatible with (and not made improbable by) being not very good at all at forming accurate beliefs about theism.[43] So these theists don't have strong R~p-evidence in support of the reliability of the atheist's beliefs on whether theism is true.

In sum, I think there are many fairly ordinary cases of theistic belief where the theist's p-evidence and Rp-evidence are strongly supportive, and her R~p-evidence is at best weakly supportive. As a result, these cases are more like the Jury Case or the Math Conference Case, where rational demotion occurs and the belief remains undefeated, than the Restaurant Case, where the belief is defeated by the recognition of peer disagreement. This is why I think theistic belief, at least of the sort I described, can be rational in the face of disagreement.[44]

3.2 Internal Rationality, External Rationality, and Satisfying Objectors to Theism

Will this response satisfy objectors to theism? Probably not. But, as with the response to skepticism about perception and memory, that isn't the goal. The goal is to consider what rationality requires in certain cases of disagreement about theism. And for the reasons given above, I think there are cases where rationality does not require theists to give up their theism. It may be that the objector to theism has different epistemic intuitions or epistemic intuitions of different strengths—about whether theistic seemings have evidential value and are veridical or about what rationality requires in the face of disagreement. But from the perspective of the theist I have in mind, the objector is mistaken not only in rejecting theism but also in endorsing epistemic intuitions that support the objection and conflict with the theist's response—a response based in part on the theist's stronger epistemic intuitions in support of her theistic

---

[43]   It's true that, in light of these virtues had by many atheists, things look better for atheism than they otherwise would. But of course theists have these same considerations in support of their own position and they have (in addition) their theistic seemings.

[44]   What about theistic belief that is not based on strong theistic seemings and is not supported by strong epistemic intuitions about the veridicality of those theistic seemings? Depending on how weak the theistic and relevant epistemic seemings are, it may be that disagreement over theism results in a defeater for such theistic belief. For more on this, see Bergmann 2015 *op. cit.* 53–5.

beliefs. In this way, the defense of theistic belief in response to the objection from disagreement over theism is similar to the Reidian defense of perceptual and memory beliefs in response to underdetermination objections targeting those beliefs: in each case the epistemic intuitions driving the objections—intuitions about principles concerning what sort of belief retraction is rationally required in certain circumstances—are ultimately overridden by stronger epistemic intuitions (in the form of higher-level seemings) about the veridicality, reliability, or rationality of first-order perceptual, memorial, and theistic seemings or beliefs.

Notice that, just as in the dispute between the radical skeptic and the Reidian defender of perception and memory, here too both sides might be internally rational. The theist could be internally rational in adopting the Reidian-style response to skeptical objectors, since such a response could be the rational response to have if one has strong theistic seemings and strong epistemic intuitions supporting the veridicality of those theistic seemings, and these are formed in epistemically appropriate ways downstream from experience. At the same time, if the objector to theism doesn't have theistic seemings or doesn't have epistemic intuitions supporting the veridicality of such seemings (or if she lacks both or if both are very weak) and these things are epistemically appropriate responses to her experience, then the internally rational response for her is skepticism about theism.

As for external rationality, if the theist's strong theistic seemings and her strong epistemic intuitions supporting their veridicality (and the things upstream from experience that produce these two kinds of seemings in the theist) are in accord with what external rationality requires, then her Reidian-style response to objectors to theism is externally rational as well, just as the Reidian response to radical skepticism is externally rational.

But what about the objector to theism? Is she doomed to external irrationality, according to the defense of theistic belief offered in this paper? Perhaps not. Granted, it may be that the objector to theism has something going epistemically wrong upstream from experience that prevents her from having epistemically appropriate theistic seemings (of sufficient strength) or from having epistemically appropriate epistemic intuitions supporting the veridicality of such theistic seemings. If so, then her skepticism would be externally irrational. But perhaps the situation of the objector to theism is more like the jurors' situation mentioned in the Jury Case. The jurors in that example weren't externally irrational in their skepticism. Instead they were quite rational. But they were mistaken because, through no epistemic deficiency on their part, they didn't have the (very good) evidence that the accused had. Moreover, they were rational (though mistaken) not to believe that the accused had good evidence. If the situation of the objector to theism is like this, then she might be both internally and externally rational in her skepticism while the theist is also internally and externally rational in her theism (just as the jurors and the accused are both internally and externally rational in their different beliefs about the guilt of the accused).

I don't mean to suggest that things are as simple in the dispute between theists and nontheists as they are for the jurors and the accused in the Jury Case. I mention that jury example here merely to emphasize that there are a variety of ways for theists and nontheists to interpret each other when considering whether the recognition of their disagreement should lead them to view themselves, or the other, as irrational.[45] My main purpose in this paper has been to explain how it is that—by relying on epistemic intuitions in the way Reidians do in response to skeptical challenges to perception and memory—theists can rationally maintain their theistic beliefs in the face of disagreement-based skeptical worries.[46]

Purdue University
bergmann@purdue.edu

[45] For more discussion of the question of how people who disagree can reasonably view each other, see Bergmann 2015 *op. cit.* 42–53 and Michael Bergmann, 'Rational Disagreement after Full Disclosure', *Episteme* 6 (2009), 336–53.

[46] For helpful comments, I want to thank the audiences at the University of Oxford, DePauw University, the University of Notre Dame, Indiana University, the University of Missouri, and the Canadian Philosophical Association meeting at the University of Ottawa. This work was supported by a research fellowship from The Experience Project funded by The John Templeton Foundation in partnership with the Center for Philosophy of Religion at the University of Notre Dame and the University of North Carolina, Chapel Hill. I'm grateful to these institutions for their support.

The Problem of Evil & Sceptical Theism

JUSTIN MCBRAYER

Abstract

The problem of evil is the problem of reconciling the existence of a perfect God with the existence of horrible things in the world. Many take this problem as a convincing reason to be an atheist. But others think that the problem can be solved. One prominent solution is called 'sceptical theism'. A sceptical theist is someone who believes in God but thinks that the problem of evil is not a real problem since humans are unable to see whether the horrible things in our world are truly pointless or else serve some greater purpose.

Do I have a coin in my pocket? On the face of it, it would seem silly for you to either think that the answer is yes or that the answer is no. You have no evidence either way. And without evidence, you should neither believe that there is a coin in my pocket nor deny it. You should be agnostic. What the case of the coin teaches us is that we need a reason to deny something. Denial isn't the 'default position.' Scepticism is.

Now consider the case of God. A theist is someone who believes that there is a God. An atheist is someone who denies that there is a God. An agnostic is someone who does neither. The agnostic neither believes that God exists nor believes that God does not exist. The agnostic is simply that: agnostic on the issue. Now this doesn't mean that the agnostic doesn't *care* about the issue. She might care a great deal. An agnostic is not necessarily passive or bored or uninterested. An agnostic is simply uncommitted.

The case of God is like the case of the coin: without evidence one way or the other, we shouldn't believe that there is a God, nor should we believe that there isn't a God. Agnosticism—not atheism—is the default position. We need evidence for theism to be a reasonable option, and we need evidence for atheism to be a reasonable option. Theists come along and present proofs, arguments, and reasons that attempt to pull us off our agnosticism towards theism. Atheists come along and do the same thing in a different direction.

There are a number of things that atheists can leverage as evidence for the non-existence of God. By far the most famous case for the non-existence of God is what people usually call the problem of evil. The idea, very quickly, is that God's existence seems

doi:10.1017/S1358246117000248

incompatible with the existence of evil, and since there is evil in the world, there must not be a God. Hence we have good evidence for atheism. Let me first say something about what I mean by 'God' and what I mean by 'evil'.

The problem of evil is not a problem for any old divine being. Showing that there is evil in the world wouldn't, for example, be considered very strong evidence against the existence of Zeus. That's because Zeus isn't a very nice guy, and so it wouldn't be surprising that a world he created would include not very nice things. However, God is supposed to be a perfect being. This perfection extends both to his moral character and to his power. So, by 'God' I mean the perfectly good, perfectly powerful being described in the great monotheisms of the world. It's *that* being that is targeted by the problem of evil.

And by 'evil' I mean any feature of the world that is bad. Pain and suffering are easy examples. If -other things being equal -the world would have been better without a certain thing, then that thing is evil on this very broad definition. And when people offer arguments from evil, they may have many different features of evil in mind. For some people, the very *existence* of any evil whatsoever constitutes good evidence against theism. For others, it's not the existence of evil, per se, but the existence of a certain *type* of evil. For example, perhaps the existence of God is compatible with minor evils like scraped knees but not horrific evils like rape or genocide. And still others insist that it's neither the mere existence nor the type of evil but the *distribution* of the evil that is good evidence against God. For example, if only evil people suffered evil things, perhaps this would be compatible with theism, but the fact that the innocent suffer is evidence against theism. Finally, certain people might think that it's the *amount* of evil that generates the strongest evidence against the existence of God. From here on, I'll use 'evil' as a general term covering all of these various aspects.

With these clarifications in hand, consider a very simple version of an argument from evil for atheism:

1. If God exists, then there is no evil in the world.
2. There IS evil in the world.
3. Therefore, God does not exist.

This argument is valid, which means if both of the assumptions are true, then the conclusion follows as a matter of logic. It's not possible for both of the assumptions to be true and the conclusion to be false. So is this a good argument?

No. Philosophers largely agree that this simple version of the argument from evil is implausible. The problem lies in the first assumption. It's easiest to introduce the problem by way of analogy. Suppose a father takes his son to the local hospital for an inoculation. The injection causes the child both fear and pain -two evils on our broad definition. Would this occasion be evidence that the father is a bad person? Of course not. We think that even though the father deliberately caused his son fear and pain, these evils are justified because of the long-term good that the inoculation secured. In other words, the evil in question is not pointless. The evil is necessary for some end result, and the end result is good enough that it compensates for the badness of the evil.

Might God be in a similar position to the father? Might certain evils be necessary for some end result and the end result be good enough that it compensates for the badness of the evil? The answer is plausibly yes. Take a simple example: building character. There is something really good about building one's own character. Not just showing up on the scene with your character already complete, but actively pushing and stretching yourself to develop character traits of your choosing. But this requires both an opportunity to fail and some hardships along the way. If you are to develop courage, you need to experience at least some times of fear and distress to do so. And this seems one of many examples of goods whose existence logically requires evils or at least the possibility of evils.

Now you might object in the following way: 'Look, God is supposed to be perfect in power. That means he can do anything. So even if it's impossible to get a certain good without a certain evil, God can do what is impossible. And so this version of the argument is sound after all.'

There is a long-standing debate among theists about whether it even makes sense to say that God can do impossible things. But fortunately, we don't have to settle this dispute here in order to see that this objection fails. Either God can do impossible things or he cannot. If he cannot, then the first assumption of this argument is mistaken for reasons just pointed out. If he can do the impossible, then the argument fails for a different reason. On this horn of the dilemma, it's no longer impossible for God to create a world filled with evils even despite the fact that he is perfectly good and perfectly powerful. In other words, the argument from evil assumes at the outset that certain things are impossible for a being like God. That's the whole point of the argument: it would be impossible to

Justin McBrayer

get a world like this if it were governed by God. But once we allow that God can do the impossible, all bets are off.

Fortunately, we can easily adjust the argument to make it stronger. Here's a more nuanced version that dodges the objection about some evils being necessary for certain goods:

1.   If God exists, then there is no *pointless* evil in the world.
2.   There IS *pointless* evil in the world.
3.   Therefore, God does not exist.

This version of the argument avoids the weakness of the first. It's not just any evil that constitutes evidence against the existence of God. It's *pointless* evil that constitutes evidence against the existence of God. A pointless evil is an evil that is *not* necessary to secure some great compensating good or prevent some worse evil. This argument grants that a sample of the evils on earth might be necessary for some compensating good. But surely not all of them are. A great many of the evils that we experience on earth seem absolutely pointless. Examples of people who suffer such pointless evils are not hard to come by: kidnapped children, earthquake survivors, people with cancer, victims of the Holocaust. Surely there is no God who would allow all of that *that*. And since it *seems* that there are many evils of this sort, there probably really are at least some. And so the second assumption is true as well.

So what can the theist say by way of reply? Historically, there have been three main options. The first is to deny the second assumption. Philosophers like St. Augustine and Spinoza think that there is no evil in the world. This position seems untenable to most contemporary thinkers. I think this response to the argument is plausible only if you deny that there are moral facts. If you truly think that nothing is right or wrong, good or bad, then, of course, the second assumption of this argument is mistaken.

The second main option is to deny the first assumption on the grounds that all of the evils in our world, despite appearances to the contrary, actually serve a greater purpose. This approach is typically called offering a theodicy or an explanation of the evils on earth. The history of philosophy is littered with various theodicies. Evil has been said to be necessary for the existence of good, knowledge of the good, free will, moral responsibility, character-building, etc. I won't say anything here about this approach other than to note that if some theodicy or set of theodicies is correct, then there are no pointless evils in the world, and this argument has a false assumption.

The third main option is the sceptical option, and it's this move that I want to focus on for the remainder of the essay. The sceptical

48

option says that we are in no epistemic position to make a call on whether or not the evils in our world are pointless. And if the sceptical option is reasonable, then we should withhold belief about assumption number two. So whereas the theodicist wants to deny assumption two, the skeptic merely wants to be agnostic about assumption two. When the skeptic is also a theist, this response to the argument from evil has come to be known as sceptical theism.

Sceptical theism has a long history in Western philosophy. The portion Jewish and Christian scripture that deals most closely with the problem of evil is the story of Job. Job was an upright man who lost everything: his family, his wealth, and his reputation. The solution to the problem—if there is one—is that Job isn't capable of fathoming the ways of God:

> Can you find out the deep things of God? Can you find out the limit of the Almighty? It is higher than heaven—what can you do? Deeper than Sheol—what can you know? (Job 11:7–8)

This same sort of scepticism can be found among philosophers in the early modern era. For example, when Descartes wrestles with a species of the problem of evil, he reasons as follows:

> As I reflect on these matters more attentively, it occurs to me first of all that it is no cause for surprise if I do not understand the reasons for some of God's actions; and there is no call to doubt his existence if I happen to find that there are other instances where I do not grasp why or how certain things were made by him. For since I now know that my own nature is very weak and limited, whereas the nature of God is immense, incomprehensible and infinite, I also know without more ado that he is capable of countless things whose causes are beyond my knowledge…there is considerable rashness in thinking myself capable of investigating the impenetrable purposes of God. (*Meditations on First Philosophy,* AT 55, Cottingham 1984 pp. 38–39)

John Locke echoes this move:

> I think it a very good Argument, to say, the infinitely wise God hath made it so: And therefore it is best. But it seems to me a little too much Confidence of our own Wisdom, to say, I think it best, and therefore God hath made it so… (*Essay*, Book I, Chapter IV, §12, Nidditch 1975, pp. 90–1)

And of course there is Hume, who perhaps puts the sceptical portion of sceptical theism most cleverly of all:

Justin McBrayer

> The great source of our mistake in the subject of God, and of the unbounded 'license to suppose' that we allow ourselves, is that we silently think of ourselves as in the place of the supreme being, and conclude that he will always behave in the way that we would find reasonable and acceptable if we were in his situation. (*Enquiry Concerning Human Understanding* §11)

Adding to this historical importance is the fact that sceptical theism has seen something of a renaissance in the last 30 years or so. Contemporary philosophers are invoking scepticism as a response to arguments from evil and doing so in ever more sophisticated ways. On the other hand, many contemporary philosophers are also offering objections to this sort of sceptical response and trying to make clear the costs of scepticism. I will offer a survey of both sides of the debate.

What can be said for sceptical theism? What reason is there for thinking that it is true and that this is the proper response to arguments from evil? I will sketch four different reasons that have been offered by contemporary sceptical theists. First, some sceptical theists have offered analogies. Suppose you were watching a chess match between two world-class champions. Unless you are a chess master yourself, you likely won't understand most of the moves made by the champions. But it would be silly to reason as follows: 'I don't see a reason for that particular move, therefore there is no good reason for that move.' Similarly, if one of the champions sacrifices a chess piece, it would silly to respond as follows: 'I don't see a compensating good that can come from that sacrifice. Therefore, there probably is no compensating good that can come from that sacrifice.' The fact of the matter is that the chess master's grasp of the game is so far above ours that we are in no position to make these kinds of judgement calls.

But then, says the sceptical theist, such is our situation vis-à-vis God. Just as a novice can't comment on whether the sacrifice of a particular chess piece is pointless, so, too, the average human can't comment on whether a particular evil in our world is pointless. And this is a reason to be sceptical about the second assumption in the argument from evil.

Second, philosophers have introduced concepts like the so-called butterfly effect to bolster our scepticism about whether any given evil is pointless. The so-called butterfly effect is when a seemingly small event leads to a much more significant outcome. For example, the flutter of a butterfly's wings in North America might start an air movement that results in a snow storm in the UK. Our knowledge of the physical world has shown us that predicting consequences over the long-term is a notoriously difficult proposition. To take one example, consider the Non-Identity Problem, a philosophical problem first made prominent in the 1980s by the British philosopher Derek Parfit. The Non-Identity Problem is the problem of determining *who* will exist in the future given that future existence is contingent on contemporary events. To take a prominent example from the literature, whether Lady Churchill went to sleep on her back or her stomach after making love to her husband would affect whether Winston Churchill or someone else was born 9 months later, and this, in turn, would have surely affected the outcome of WWII which would have surely affected who would exist in the year 2015.

Given this complexity, some philosophers urge caution in assuming that any particular evil is pointless. Remember: if an evil was necessary for a compensating good down the road, then it's not a pointless evil. And since the long-term consequences of our actions and various states of affairs are so hard to predict, epistemic humility requires that we refrain from classifying current events as ultimately pointless.

Third, philosophers have offered what are called sensitivity constraints on evidence. The most famous comes from an American philosopher named Stephen Wykstra who argues for a condition on when the non-existence of evidence constitutes evidence of non-existence. Wykstra thinks that a lack of evidence for something is evidence that there really is no such thing *only if* it's also true that if there were evidence for it, we would likely be aware of it. For example, suppose I ask you if there are any elephants in this room. You could look around and - seeing no elephants - conclude that there are no elephants in the room. This makes sense because if there would have been an elephant, you would very likely see it. So your non-evidence counts as evidence. But suppose I ask you if there are any germs in this room. You could look around and -seeing no germs - conclude that there are no germs in the room. But this doesn't make sense, and the epistemic principle in question explains why. If there were germs in the room, your evidence would look exactly the same to you. So in this case, your non-evidence does not count as evidence.

Hopefully the connection to sceptical theism is now perfectly clear. The question is whether the goods that might compensate for the evils we experience are more like elephants or germs. Some philosophers have argued that they are more like germs. Even if they existed, we are unlikely to be aware of compensating goods in a wide range of cases, and so the fact that we can see no compensating good for an evil does not license the conclusion that there is no such good. Hence we have no reason to endorse the second assumption of the argument from evil.

Fourth, and finally, philosophers like the American Philosopher Michael Bergmann, have invoked inductive scepticism in defense of sceptical theism. The basic idea is similar to the last point about sensitivity. It is reasonable to make an inductive inference from what we know to what we don't only when we have good reason for thinking that our sample is representative. For example, if I tell you that all thirty of my water samples of the Thames River are polluted, should you conclude that it is likely that the Thames River is polluted? Well, no. You'll want to know where my samples were taken from. If all thirty came from the same exact location just downstream of London, then you shouldn't make any broad inferences on the basis of that data. However, if I tell you that the thirty samples came from the entire length of the river at randomly assigned locations, then this seems like pretty good evidence that the Thames River is polluted.

So how does this connect to sceptical theism? Consider the range of goods you are familiar with, the range of evils you are familiar with, and the range of connections between goods and evils that you are familiar with. Are you sure that your sample is representative in all three cases? Some philosophers think that you should doubt this. Maybe there are a lot more types of goods, evils or connections between the two than we can fathom. And unless we have a reason to think that our sample is representative, we shouldn't make any inductive inferences about whether the evils in our world are truly pointless.

Needless to say, sceptical theism has its detractors, both inside and outside of theism. What can be said against sceptical theism? What reason is there for thinking that it is false or an improper response to arguments from evil? I will sketch three different objections that contemporary philosophers have offered to sceptical theism.

First, some philosophers are concerned that sceptical theism seems to entail a view called ethical consequentialism. Ethical consequentialism is the view that right and wrong are solely functions of the consequences of actions. If an action has good enough consequences, then it will be the right thing to do. In slogan form: the ends justify the means.

Suppose someone says that the death of a child in a car accident is a pointless evil. The sceptical theist responds by pointing out that -for all we know -this death was necessary to secure some great good or stave off some really bad evil. But this seems to commit the sceptical theist to the view that *anything* is, in principle, morally permissible so long as it produces enough good in the end. And that sounds like ethical consequentialism.

Now whether this implication is a bad thing depends on one's view of ethics. In point of fact, a great many professional philosophers are utilitarians which means that they endorse a species of ethical consequentialism. But other philosophers have been convinced that there are absolute moral prohibitions -things that are wrong no matter the consequences. If there are absolute moral prohibitions, then a new form of the argument from evil could be constructed showing that at least some of the evils that occur are violations of these absolute moral prohibitions. If that could be done, sceptical theism would be impotent as a response.

Second, sceptical theism might backfire on theists. Remember, sceptical theists are sceptical about our ability to determine whether any apparently pointless evil is genuinely pointless. God is so far above our level, that we're unable to grasp his ways. But then won't this scepticism 'bleed over' into the life of a theist? Take one of the most famous arguments for theism, the argument from design. The idea is roughly that our world is so perfectly designed that it must have had a powerful and provident creator. But, to take the sceptical quote from Hume seriously, when we imagine what the world would look like if it were created by a powerful and provident creator, aren't we silently thinking of ourselves as in the place of the supreme being, and concluding that he will always behave in the way that we would find reasonable and acceptable if we were in his situation? Maybe we should be agnostic about what a good world would look like, and if so, we should be agnostic about a crucial assumption in the argument from design.

Or to take a more practical example, how do we know that any of the world's scriptures are authentic or any religious experience veridical? After all, if the ends justify the means, then how are we to trust any putative divine revelation? If we say that it is an absolute prohibition that God deceive us (as Descartes held), then the earlier objection to sceptical theism applies. On the other hand, if lying is morally permissible given good enough consequences, then sceptical theism seems to undercut the basis for our trust in God's communications with humans.

Third, and finally, taking sceptical theism seriously seems to impose a kind of moral paralysis on the part of the skeptic. An example makes this clear. Suppose you are hiking in the forest and come upon a child drowning in a pond. Should you save her? You might think the initial answer is a resounding yes: you have a moral obligation to aid the drowning child. But suppose your sceptical theism kicks in. It's possible that there is a good reason to let her drown. After all, for all you know, this child could be the next Hitler! Now that may sound far-fetched, but remember: God's ways are not our ways, and compensating goods and evils are hard for us to see. So the mere fact that we can see no good reason to let the child drown doesn't make it likely that there is no such reason. Sceptical theists seem to be stuck: no matter how they reason about the drowning child case, there is no satisfactory explanation for what one ought to do. And that is a high price to pay to avoid the argument from evil for atheism.

Of course, sceptical theists have offered responses to each of these objections. But surveying these responses is beyond the scope of the present project which has been to offer and motivate a clear form of an argument from evil, explain the sceptical response to the argument, and offer reasons both for and against taking this response seriously.

Fort Lewis College, the public liberal arts
college for the state of Colorado
jpmcbrayer@fortlewis.edu

Skeptical theism and Skepticism About the External World and Past

STEPHEN LAW

Abstract

Skeptical theism is a popular - if not universally theistically endorsed - response to the evidential problem of evil. Skeptical theists question how we can be in a position to know God lacks God-justifying reason to allow the evils we observe. In this paper I examine a criticism of skeptical theism: that the skeptical theists skepticism re divine reasons entails that, similarly, we cannot know God lacks God-justifying reason to deceive us about the external world and the past. This in turn seems to supply us with a defeater for all our beliefs regarding the external world and past? Critics argue that either the skeptical theist abandon their skeptical theism, thereby resurrecting the evidential argument from evil, or else they must embrace seemingly absurd skeptical consequences, including skepticism about the external world and past. I look at various skeptical theist responses to this critique and find them all wanting.

1. Skeptical Theism

Evidential arguments from evil often take something like the following form:

> If God exists, gratuitous evil does not exist.
> Gratuitous evil exists.
> Therefore, God does not exist

By 'God' I mean a being that is omnipotent, omniscient, and supremely good. Most theists accept that God will allow an evil if there is an God-justifying reason for him to do so - e.g. if that evil is required by God to secure some compensating good or to prevent some equally bad or worse evil. A 'gratuitous evil', by contrast, is an evil there is no God-justifying reason to permit.

By a 'God-justifying reason' I mean a reason that would actually justify God in permitting that evil. Suppose I can save a child drowning in a river by reaching out to him from the bank with a piece of splintered wood. I decide against doing so because I might get a splinter from the wood. The risk of getting a splinter gives me *some* reason not to save the child using that piece of wood, but of course it's hardly an adequate reason. If God exists, then presumably he

doi:10.1017/S1358246117000285   © The Royal Institute of Philosophy and the contributors 2017

Royal Institute of Philosophy Supplement **81** 2017

Stephen Law

has not just *some* reason to permit the evils we observe, but adequate reason - reason that justifies him in permitting those evils.

Further, for an evil to be gratuitous, there needs to be no *all-things-considered* good reason for God allow it. An all-things-considered good reason is a reason that, when all factors are taken into account, justifies the relevant course of action (or inaction). Suppose I see child A is about to walk into some nettles. I have good reason to prevent her doing so: she'll get badly stung. That 's a reason that would justify me in stopping her. Still, all-things-considered it might be better if I *didn't* stop child A and instead stopped child B whom I can see is about to walk in front of a car (assuming I can't do both). God may similarly allow evils he has reasons to prevent, including evils he'd be justified in preventing. What God presumably won't allow is evils he is *all-things-considered* justified in preventing. Henceforth, when I discuss 'God-justifying reasons' for doing x, I'll mean reasons that all-things-considered justify God in doing x.

Why suppose the second premise of the above argument is true? A so-called 'noseeum' inference has been offered in its support.[1] It is suggested that if we cannot think of any God-justifying reason for an evil we observe, then we are justified in concluding that no such reason exists.

One obvious way to challenge this evidential argument from evil is to try actually to *identify reasons* why God might be justified in allowing the evils we observe, thereby showing that the evils are not, after all, gratuitous. Various attempts have been made. Some suggest that much of the evil we observe (in particular, the moral evils - the morally bad things we do of our own volition) can be explained as a result of God giving us *free will*. Some suggest that many natural evils - such as the natural diseases and disasters which cause great suffering to the sentient inhabitants of this planet - can be explained as a result of the operation of natural laws that are required for compensating or still greater goods (e.g. perhaps the tectonic plate movements that cause earthquakes and thus much suffering are necessary for life to emerge in the first place, say). Some suggest that many evils are divinely justified because they are for character-building or 'soul making' purposes. Just as a parent will permit their child repeatedly to fall off their bike and graze their knees given it's only by enduring such repeated falls that the child can gain not only the good of being

---

[1]   Wykstra dubbed such arguments 'noseeum' inferences. See his 'Rowe's noseeum arguments from evil' in D. Howard-Snyder, (ed.) *The Evidential Argument from Evil* (Indiana: Indiana University Free Press, 1996) 126–50.

56

able to ride their bike but also the justified sense of achievement that comes with it, so God will permit us to graze our metaphorical knees given that it's only by such means that we can become better people.

However, even many theists accept that these various explanations of why God would allow such evils are not only individually, but collectively, inadequate. I'd suggest that, for the two hundred thousand year history of human beings, the death of on average around half of every generation of children (usually in a pretty horrific way), with all the child and parental suffering and grief that that involves, is on the face of it, *very* difficult for theists to explain in any of the above ways, as is the hundreds of millions of years of horrific non-human suffering that occurred before we humans showed up.

The skeptical theist takes a rather different approach to the evidential argument from evil. Rather than try to identify the reasons why God is justified in allowing observed evils, the skeptical theist suggests that our inability to identify such reasons is not a sound basis for concluding that no such reasons exist.

The skeptical theist challenges the noseeum inference offered in support of premise 2. True, we are sometimes justified in inferring that there are no Fs given that there do not appear to be any Fs. I am justified in believing there are no elephants in my garage given there do not, looking in from the street, appear to be any there. But, the skeptical theist, points out, noseeum inferences aren't always sound. I am not justified in supposing there are no insects in my garage just because there do not, looking in from the street, appear to be any. Given my perceptual limitations, there could, for all I know, still be insects present. But then, suggests the skeptical theist, given *our* cognitive limitations, there could, for all we know, be God-justifying reasons for the evils we observe despite our inability to think of any.

We might think of those goods of which we are aware and those evils of which we are aware (and the entailment relations between them of which we are aware) as the tip of an iceberg of reasons. According to the skeptical theist, we don't know how much of this iceberg is accessible to us or how representative the tip is. But then, given our cognitive limitations, we cannot conclude from the fact that the part of the iceberg to which we have cognitive access contains no God-justifying reason to allow the evils we observe that it is probable (or even more probable then not) that there is no such reason in what remains. We are, insists the skeptical theist, simply *in the dark* about whether such a reason exists.

So, the skeptical theist maintains that, even if we can't identify any God-justifying reasons for the evils we observe, we are not justified in concluding that gratuitous evils exist. But then the evidential argument fails. Let's call the above skeptical theist attempt to block the noseeum inference the 'anti-noseeum argument'.[2]

Note that skeptical theism involves to claims: (i) theism, and (ii) skepticism regarding our ability to think of the reasons that might God justify God in allowing observed evils. Also note than even an atheist might embrace the skeptical part of skeptical theism. While failing to believe in God, they may nevertheless accept that, for all they know, there is a reason that would justify God, *if* he existed, in allowing the evils we observe.

Skeptical theism has been embraced and developed by several philosophers of religion, including Alvin Plantinga who, in response to the evidential problem of evil, says:

> ...from the theistic perspective there is little or no reason to think that God would have a reason for a particular evil state of affairs only if we had a pretty good idea of what that reason might be. On the theistic conception, our cognitive powers, as opposed to God's, are a bit slim for that. God might have reasons we cannot so much as understand.[3]

Michael Bergmann, a leading defender of skeptical theism, puts the objection thus:

> The fact that humans can't think of any God-justifying reason for permitting and evil, doesn't make it likely that there are no such reasons; this is because if God existed, God's mind would be far greater than our minds so it wouldn't be surprising if God has reasons we weren't able to think of.[4]

---

[2] I note in passing that a version of the evidential argument from evil might still succeed even if the claim that gratuitous evil exists cannot be justified. Suppose that for a belief to be justified, it's epistemic probability must be at least 0.85 (if one bullet is placed in six chamber revolver, the chamber is spun and the gun about to be fired, the probability it won't fire is 0.85, but intuitively I am not justified in thinking the gun won't fire). But then suppose the probability that gratuitous evil exists is 0.84. Then the probability that gratuitous evil exists is not sufficient for belief that it exists to be justified. Nevertheless, a probability of 0.84 is sufficient to lower theism's probability below credibility. My thanks to Trent Dougherty for flagging this.

[3] A. Plantinga, 'Epistemic probability and evil', in D. Howard-Snyder (ed.) op cit. 1996, 69–96, 73.

[4] M. Bergmann, 'Commonsense skeptical theism' in K. Clark and M. Rea (eds.) *Science, Religion, and Metaphysics: New Essays on the Philosophy of Alvin Plantinga* (Oxford: Oxford University Press, 2012), 9–30, 11.

According to Bergmann, the skeptical theist's skepticism (detached from their theism) includes as a main ingredient endorsement of such skeptical theses as:

ST1: We have no good reason for thinking that the possible goods we know of are representative of the possible goods there are.

ST2: We have no good reason for thinking the possible evils we know of are representative of the possible evils there are.

ST3: We have no good reason for thinking that the entailment relations we know of between possible goods and the permission of possible evils are representative of the entailment relations there are between possible goods and the permission of possible evils.

ST4: We have no good reason for thinking that the total moral value or disvalue we perceive in certain complex states of affairs accurately reflects the total moral value or disvalue they really have.

Bergmann maintains that, given the truth of ST1-ST4, we are in the dark about whether there exist God-justifying reasons to permit the evils we observe. Thus the evidential argument from evil fails.

As McBrayer and Swenson[5], two defenders of skeptical theism, point out, the skeptical theist's anti-noseeum argument applies, not just with respect to God-justifying reasons to allow or bring about evils, but with respect to God-justifying reasons to allow or bring about *anything at all*. If skeptical theism is true, we cannot, from the fact that we are unable to think of a God-justifying reason for God to bring about or allow so-and-so, justifiably conclude that no such reason exists.

Notice however that the skeptical theist need not - and arguably should not - be *too* skeptical regarding knowledge divine reasons.

Note, first of all, that skeptical theism allows theists can legitimately draw *some* conclusions about divine reasons given what they observe of the world. For example, they can legitimately infer from the fact that Bert's house burnt down last night, that God, if exists, had an adequate reason to permit that. Here is an inference from an observed evil to a conclusion concerning divine reasons that *is* permitted by the skeptical theist.

[5]   McBrayer, J. and Swenson, P. 'Skepticism and the argument from divine hiddenness', *Religious Studies* **48** (2012), 129–150.

Further, note that skeptical theists can allow that we can also know at least some of God's reasons by means of some form of direct, divine revelation. Perhaps God can and indeed has directly revealed to some of us what his reasons are, and indeed what reasons he lacks. In which case, *no inference* - let alone a noseeum inference - *at all* is required in order for us to possess knowledge of both the existence and the absence of God-justifying reasons.

So skeptical theists can, and usually do, allow human knowledge of divine reasons. They're merely skeptical about our ability to think of the reasons God might have for creating or allowing the evils - and indeed the various other things - we observe. They question only the 'noseeum' inference from (i) we can't think of any such reasons, to (ii) no such reasons exist.

Note that skeptical theists disagree over whether the evils we observe provide some evidence against theism. Some insist the evils we observe provide no evidence *at all* against theism. Others allow that observed evils may provide *some* evidence against theism. They merely insist that - given the shaky nature of any noseeum inference from observed evils to the conclusion that no God-justifying reason for those evils exists - what evidence there is falls short of allowing us justifiably to conclude that the world contains gratuitous evil and that consequently theism is false.

2. Skeptical theism and knowledge of God's goodness

As McBrayer and Swenson acknowledge[6], skeptical theism also appears to threaten a number of arguments for the existence of the God of traditional monotheism. How are we to know that, not only is there an omnipotent and omniscient creator of the universe (a lower case 'g' god, if you like) but this creator is *good* (the upper case 'G' God)? According to McBrayer and Swenson, *not* by observing the universe and drawing conclusions about divine goodness on that basis. For if skeptical theism is true, we are as much in the dark about whether a good God would, or would not, bring about the goods we observe as we are about whether he would, or would not, bring about the evils we observe. But then observed goods are no more evidence for a good God then observed evils are evidence against.

Michael Bergmann, another proponent of skeptical theism, concurs that arguments for divine goodness based on identifying

---

[6]   McBrayer and Swenson (2012) op cit.

some feature of the universe as an all-considered good are under-mined by skeptical theism. According to Bergmann, anyone who supposes the order we see in the natural world or the joy we witness in people's lives give us reason to think that there is a benevo-lent God who is the cause of such things is failing to take into account the lessons of skeptical theism.[7]

This isn't to say that skeptical theism has the consequence that we should be skeptical about the existence of a good God. As Bergmann points out: 'We needn't conclude ... that the skeptical theist's skepti-cism is inconsistent with every way of arguing for the existence of a good God'[8]. Alternative ways by which we might come justifiably to believe in the existence of God might perhaps involve other forms of inference invulnerable to skeptical theism (e.g. an onto-logical or moral argument), or divine revelation.

3. The Pandora's Box Problem

One leading response to skeptical theism is to show that *it opens up a skeptical Pandora's Box*: it entails forms of skepticism that even the theists finds implausible and unacceptable. In particular, skeptical theism appears to require we also embrace *skepticism about the exter-nal world and the past*.

Consider the following familiar example of an *undercutting defea-ter*. I am watching, through a window, a series of widgets pass by on an assembly line. The widgets clearly look red. I come to believe the widgets are red on that basis. Presumably, given the widgets appear perceptually red to me, then it is *ceteris paribus*, rea-sonable for me to believe the widgets are red. However, suppose I am then told, by someone who has previously proved to be a reliable source of information, that the widgets are lit by a special defect-re-vealing light, a light that makes even non-red things look red. Is it *still* reasonable for me to believe the widgets are red?

Intuitively not. Why not? Because I now have good reason to think that the method by which I acquired the original belief is, in the circumstances in which I formed it, not to be trusted.

What, exactly, is 'defeated' in such cases? That's arguable. Some maintain that *knowledge* is lost in such cases. Even if the widgets are

---

[7]   M. Bergmann, 'Skeptical Theism and the Problem of Evil' in T. Flint and M. Rea (eds.) *Oxford Handbook to Philosophical Theology*, (Oxford: Oxford University Press, 2009) 374–399.

[8]   Bergmann, (2009) op cit.

Stephen Law

red (and I've been misled about that defect-revealing light), I don't *know* they are red. Others are inclined to think that knowledge need not be lost in such cases, but that at the very least *reasonable belief* is lost. Lasonen Aarnio[9], for example, argues that in such cases knowledge may be retained (e.g. if knowledge belief is acquired by means of a safe method, and the method employed - visual perception in this case - is indeed safe) but that reasonable belief is lost. According to Lasonen Aarnio, the reason reasonable belief is lost is that someone who continues to maintain their belief that the widgets are red even after having received the new information about the defect-revealing light, has embarked upon a belief-forming strategy that is not knowledge-conducive. Lasonen Aarnio suggests reasonableness

> is at least largely a matter of managing one's beliefs through the adoption of policies that are generally knowledge conducive, thereby manifesting dispositions to know and avoid false belief across a wide range of normal cases. Subjects who stubbornly stick to their beliefs in the face of new evidence manifest dispositions that are bad given the goal of knowledge or even of true belief.[10]

Someone who continues to believe even after acquiring such new evidence about the unreliability of the method by which they formed their belief will likely end up believing many falsehoods. I shall assume that Lasonen Aarnio is correct: whether or not knowledge is necessarily 'defeated' in such cases, reasonable belief is. Call such defeaters *rationality defeaters* (leaving it open whether knowledge is also lost).

But then doesn't skeptical theism generate a rationality defeater for beliefs regarding the external world and past? Given that it appears to me both that I ate toast for breakfast this morning and that there is an orange on the table in front of me, it is presumably reasonable for me to believe I ate toast for breakfast and that there is an orange before me. But if I now learn that, (i) God exists, and (ii) for all I know, there is a God-justifying reason for God to deceive me about these things, then, runs the objection, I can no longer reasonably believe I had toast for breakfast or that there is an orange there. For skeptical theism blocks any attempt to justify the belief that there are unlikely to be such God-justifying reasons by means of a noseeum inference:

[9]   M. Lasonen Aarnio, M. 'Unreasonable Knowledge', *Philosophical Perspectives*, 24 (2010) 1–21.
[10]   Laasonen Aarnio (2010) op cit. 2.

'I can't think of a good reason why God would deceive me in that way, therefore there probably is no such reason.' But then skeptical theism would seem to have the consequence that, for all I know, God does indeed have a good reason to deceive me in this way and is deceiving me for that reason. Just as learning about that defect-revealing light provides me with an rationality defeater for my belief that the widgets are red - I should be skeptical about whether or not the widgets are red - so learning that (i) and (ii) generates a rationality defeater for my beliefs about the external world and past - I should be skeptical about the external world and past.

Of course, most theists reject the view that we should be skeptical about the external world and past. They believe we can reasonably hold beliefs about both. But if their skeptical theism requires that they embrace such a broad skeptical position, then it appears they must either embrace that broad skeptical position, or else abandon their skeptical theism, thereby resurrecting the evidential argument from evil.

Note that other beliefs also appear to be thrown into doubt by skeptical theism. Take a theist's belief that their religion - Christianity, let's say - is true. Skeptical theism appears to entail that, for all they know, there is a reason that justifies God, if he exists, in deceiving them about Christianity (maybe the truth of Christianity is something about which God wishes to trick us in order to achieve some, to us unknown, greater good). But then it seems skeptical theism provides our Christian with rationality defeater for their Christian beliefs. They should, it seems, be skeptical about Christianity, just as they should be skeptical about the external world and past.

Note that, even if disbelievers (those who believe there is no God) do accept the skeptical part of skeptical theism (they endorse the thought that they are in no position to know whether there's a reason that justifies God, if he exists, in deceiving them), they don't end up falling into the same skeptical swamp. For, on their view, there exists no such God, and thus no such deceiver.

Commonsensism

In response to the Pandora's Box Objection, some insist that, yes, we cannot by means of a noseeum inference, conclude God lacks a reason to deceive us about the external world and past - i.e. we cannot think of a reason why God would deceive us about the external world and past; therefore there probably is no such reason. However, while *that* way of establishing that God lacks a reason to so deceive us is blocked,

Stephen Law

other ways of knowing that he lacks such a reason may remain. Perhaps, given there are these other ways of knowing about the external world and the past (ways that don't rely on any noseeum inference regarding God's reasons), skeptical theism constitutes no threat to such knowledge.

For example, Michael Bergmann, in response to the Pandora's Box objection, appeals to what he calls *commonsensism*.

> *Commonsensism*: the view that (a) it is clear that we know many of the most obvious things we take ourselves to know (this includes the truth of simple perceptual, memory, introspective, mathematical, logical, and moral beliefs) and that (b) we also know (if we consider the question) that we are not in some skeptical scenario in which we are radically deceived in these beliefs.[11]

Bergmann then considers Sally, a hypothetical agnostic who believes ST1-ST4 but who also signs up to commonsensism. According to Bergmann, given Sally's commonsensism, especially clause (b),

> she knows, in addition to the fact that she has hands, that's she's not a brain in a vat being deceived into thinking she has hands. And similarly, she knows that if God exists, then God doesn't have an all-things-considered good reason for making it seems that she has hands when in fact she doesn't. She knows this despite her endorsement of ST1-ST4... By endorsing ST1-ST4, Sally is committing herself to the view that we don't know, *just by reflecting on possible goods, possible evils, the entailment relations between them, and their seeming value or disvalue,* what God's reasons might be. But it doesn't follow that we have no way *at all* of knowing anything about what reasons God might have for doing things... In general, for all the things we commonsensically know to be true, we know that God, (if God exists) didn't have an all-things-considered good reason to make them false.[12]

Note the intriguing move made here: from the fact that we do know (other than by means of a noseeum inference) about the external world and past, we can infer that God, if he exists, has no God-justifying reason to deceive us about the external world and past. A similar move is made by Beaudoin[13] who, in response the

---

[11] M. Bergmann (2012) op cit. 10.
[12] M. Bergmann (2012) op cit. 15.
[13] J. Beaudoin, J. 'Skepticism and the skeptical theist', *Faith and Philosophy*, **22** (2005) 42–56.

thought that skeptical theism entails that, for all we know, God actualised **s**: an old-looking universe that is in truth just five minutes old (this being the universe we inhabit), suggests that while we cannot infer God lacks a reason to so deceive us about the age of the universe from the fact that we cannot think of any such reason, insists that nevertheless we can infer God lacks such a reason from the fact that we do, in fact, know the universe is older than that. Beaudoin draws the following analogy:

> Suppose I know nothing about Smith's honesty, or lack thereof. For all I know, Smith is an inveterate liar. Now I claim to believe something (P) Smith told me, but not on the basis of Smith's telling me; instead I've confirmed with my own eyes that (P). Clearly in this case it wouldn't do for someone to challenge the rationality of my belief by pointing out that for all I know Smith is a liar; my belief that (P) isn't based on Smith's testimony.[14]

Similarly, then, says Beaudoin, we may yet know the universe is old, not by way of a noseeum inference to a conclusion about God's lacking reason to deceive us concerning its age, but in some other way. Perhaps, says Beaudoin,

> there is some theologically neutral, telling philosophical argument for rejecting skepticism about the past. If there is, then on this basis the skeptical theist can conclude that God has no [morally sufficient reason] for actualizing **s**, since he has not actualized it.[15]

I call this the *Bergmann/Beaudoin response* to the Pandora's Box objection to skeptical theism.

I don't believe the Bergmann/Beaudoin response succeeds in disarming The Pandora's Box objection. Consider another putative example of rationality defeat, which I call *Olly's Orange*[16].

Olly's Orange

Suppose I seem very clearly to see an orange on the table in front of me. Other things being equal, it seems reasonable for me to believe

---

[14]   Beaudoin 2005 op cit. 44.
[15]   Beaudoin 2005, op cit. 45.
[16]   I previously used this example in S. Law, 'The Pandora's Box Objection to Skeptical Theism' in *International Journal of Religious Studies*, **78** (2015) 285–299.

that there is an orange there. Suppose I do consequently form the belief that there's an orange there. However, I now come by new information. I am given excellent reason to believe (i) that someone called Olly is present who is in possession of an amazing holographic projector capable of projecting onto the table before me an entirely convincing-looking image of an orange, and (ii) that I am entirely in the dark about whether Olly is now projecting such an image. Given this new information, is it reasonable for me to continue to believe there's an orange before me?

I think the answer is pretty clearly no: it's not reasonable for me to continue to hold my belief about the orange. I should, given this new information, withhold belief - be skeptical - about whether there's an orange there.

Now in response to my skepticism, suppose someone argues like so. It is *generally* reasonable for us to trust our senses and memories. As Bergmann notes, 'it is clear we know many of the most obvious things we take ourselves to know (this includes the truth of simple perceptual [and] memory…beliefs).' In particular, such skeptic-busting principles as the following are plausible:

> P1. If it clearly perceptually looks to me as if S is the case, then, *ceteris paribus*, it is reasonable for me to believe that S is the case.

> P2. If someone tells me that S is the case, then, *ceteris paribus*, it is reasonable for me to believe S is the case.

(The *ceteris paribus* clauses here will obviously include where you also have good reason to distrust your senses or the testifier. E.g. it's not reasonable to believe a stick is bent given it looks bent when half immersed in this glass of water if I have good reason to suppose that even straight sticks look bent under those circumstances.) But then, given it clearly looks to me as if there is an orange on the table before me, it *is* reasonable to believe there is an orange there. This is something I can 'commonsensically' take myself to know. And, given I can reasonably believe that there is an orange there, so I can reasonably believe I am not being deceived by Olly etc. about there being an orange there. So I am *not* in the dark about whether Olly is using his projector. I can reasonably believe (and indeed know) that he is not.

I think it is pretty clear that something has gone wrong with this Bergmann-Beaudion-style boot-strapping justification for supposing I can reasonably believe there is an orange there and thus reasonably believe Olly is not deceiving me.

Note, in particular, that even if principles such as P1 and P2 are correct, the *ceteris paribus* clause surely kicks in when I am presented with new evidence that my senses (or the testifier) are not to be trusted in the circumstances in which I formed the belief. *Ceteris paribus*, I can reasonably there's an orange there if that's how it looks. But not given I have good grounds to accept, and do accept, the new information that (i) Olly is present and easily capable of deceiving me, and (ii) for all I know Olly is in fact deceiving me. Under *these* circumstances, it seems I possess a rationality defeater for my perceptually-based belief. I reasonably consider myself 'commonsensically' to know there's an orange present.

But then similarly, irrespective of whether it is, *ceteris paribus*, reasonable for us to believe that things are perceptually as they appear to be, given I have good grounds to accept, and do accept, that (i) there is a being easily capable of deceiving me perceptually, and (ii) for all I know this being is deceiving me, then I have a rationality defeater for my perceptually based beliefs.

Hence the Bergmann/Beaudoin response to the Pandora's Box objection appears to fail.

Can we know God is no deceiver?

Another response to the Pandora's Box objection is to argue that we can, independently, know God is no deceiver because we can know that God is good and a good God is no deceiver. In his *Third Meditation*, Descartes offers an argument for this claim. He says God 'cannot be a deceiver, since it is a dictate of the natural light that all fraud and deception spring from some defect', and God is without defect. However, Maitzen[17] (2009) points out that while fraud and deception flow from some defective situation (a terrorist about to explode a bomb who can only be thwarted by deception, for example) it does not follow that 'fraud and deception are defective *responses* to that situation'.[18] Hobbes similalrly points out, in response to Descartes, that it

> ... is the common belief that no fault is committed by medical men who deceive sick people for health's sake, nor by parents who mislead their children for their good ... M. Descartes must therefore look to the this proposition, God can in no case deceive us, taken universally, and see whether it is true...[19]

[17] S. Maitzen, S. Skeptical theism and moral obligation. *International Journal of the Philosophy of Religion*, **65** (2009) 93–103.

[18] S. Maitzen, op cit. 97.

[19] E. Haldane, E, and G.R.T. Ross (trans.), *The Philosophical Works of Descartes*, Volume II (Cambridge: Cambridge University Press, 1967) 78.

Where a reason sufficient to justify us in engaging in deceive exists, our engaging in such deception does not require there be any defect in us. So why does God's similarly engaging in such deception require there be some defect in him? The New Testament also contains passages suggesting God engages in deliberate deception. St. Paul describes God as sending some people 'a powerful delusion, leading them to believe what is false.' (2nd Thessalonians 2:11). So the Cartesian thought that God is no deceiver is Biblically challenged, too.

Is being 'in the dark' about whether God has reason to deceive us sufficient to justify skepticism?

Here's another response to the Pandora's Box problem.

Suppose Paul tells me, with seeming sincerity, that he had an apple for breakfast. I have only just met Paul and don't know anything about him. Nevertheless, I believe him. Is it reasonable for me to believe him?

Well, am I not *in the dark* about whether Paul has reason to deceive me about his breakfast this morning? Paul is a complete stranger to me. I know nothing about his background or his motives. So, *for all I know*, Paul has some all-things-considered good reason to deceive me about his breakfast. Should I not then withhold judgement about - be skeptical - about whether Paul had an apple for breakfast?

Skepticsm in this case seems absurd. Surely, despite the fact that I am in the dark about Paul's motives and the reasons he might have to deceive me, it's reasonable for me to just take Paul's word for it about his having an apple for breakfast.

Note that principle P2 explains why it's reasonable for me to take Paul's word for it about the apple: *ceteris paribus* it is reasonable for me to take testimony at face value; hence it's reasonable in this case. Notice that if I *were* sceptical in this case, then consistency would require I be sceptical about a great deal since much of what I believe is based on the testimony of folk not well known to me - folk who, for all I know, have reason to deceive me.

Hence, a defender of skeptical theism may insist, the mere fact that I am in the dark about whether God has good reason to deceive me - the fact that for all I know he has reason to deceive me - does not entail that I cannot reasonable believe God's testimony, or indeed my senses and memory.

To assess this response to the Pandora's Box Objection, we need to get clearer about what being 'in the dark' and 'for all I know' mean here. When sceptical theists say we are 'in the dark' about whether there exist God-justifying reasons for God to allow the evils we observe - that 'for all we know' such reasons exist - they re-articulate this thought in a variety of ways. Some speak of probability. They say that the probability of God having such a reason is *inscrutable* to us, by which they mean that we cannot reasonably assign any probability to God's having such a reason: neither high, nor low, nor middling. Others speak of probability but say only that we cannot assign a *low* probability to God's having such a reason.

If we now turn to the case of Paul, I think it is pretty clear that while I might, correctly, say 'for all I know' Paul has a reason to deceive me - that I am 'in the dark' about whether Paul has reason to deceive me - the sense with which these expressions are being used is not that with which they are used by the skeptical theist.

It's actually very reasonable for me to believe that Paul lacks a reason to deceive me because, after all, Paul is a human being, and I know a great deal about human beings generally, including the kind of reasons that lead them to deceive others, the extent to which they can survey the range of reasons that would motivate them to deceive others, and so on. Given all this information about human beings and their reasons to deceive, it's reasonable for me to believe that, while Paul might have reason to deceive me, the probability he actually has such a reason is low. But then that low probability doesn't give me a rationality defeater for my belief that Paul had an apple for breakfast given only that he told me so. True, I am, in a sense, 'in the dark' about whether Paul has such a reason - 'for all I know' Paul has such a reason - but only in the very weak sense that it's possible that he has such a reason - I can't entirely rule out his possessing such a reason. I can still reasonably assign a *low* probability to his having such a reason.

When we turn to a skeptical theist's claim that we are 'in the dark' about whether there are God-justifying reasons for observed evils, on the other hand, the claim is that the probability God has such a reason is *inscrutable* and/or is at least *not* low. If we could reasonably suppose the probability of there being such a reason was low, then perhaps we might still reasonably believe there's no such reason, and thus reasonably believe that the evils we observe are gratuitous. So, if their response to the evidential problem of evil is to succeed, the skeptical theist's sense of our being 'in the dark' re the existence of certain God justifying reasons needs to be a very different sense to that which applies in the case of Paul's potential reasons to deceive me.

But then if it's in this stronger sense that we are supposedly 'in the dark' regarding the existence of God-justifying reasons of observed

Stephen Law

evils, then it will also be in this stronger sense that we are 'in the dark' regarding the existence of God-justifying reasons for God to deceive us about the external world and past. But then the analogy drawn between our 'being in the dark' about God's having good reason to deceive us and my being 'in the dark' about Paul's having good reason to deceive me fails. Even if it is reasonable for me to trust Paul, notwithstanding my being 'in the dark' about his having good reason to deceive me, it does not follow that it's reasonable for me to trust God, notwithstanding my being 'in the dark' about God's having good reason to deceive me. It seems I really do have reason to distrust God since I cannot - as I can in the case of Paul - *reasonably assign a low probability to God's having good reason to deceive me.*

Note, by the way, that in *Olly's Orange*, for my analogy to appropriate, I must be 'in the dark' in the strong sense about whether Olly has turned his projector on. That's to say, I cannot reasonably assign a low probability to Olly's having turned his projector on. Under those circumstances, it appears I do have a rationality defeater for my belief there's an orange before me.

Conclusion

Perhaps the Pandora's Box objection to skeptical theism can successfully be dealt with, but it seems clear to me that none of the above attempted solutions succeed. In which case, the sceptical theist does appear to be faced with a dilemma: (i) maintain their sceptical theism in order to deal with the evidential argument from evil, but then lose reasonable belief in the external world, the past, and Christianity (or Islam, or whatever), or (ii) abandon their skeptical theism, leaving them to again face the evidential problem from evil.

Heythrop College, University of London
think@royalinstitutephilosophy.org

Sceptical Theism, the Butterfly Effect and Bracketing the Unknown

ALEXANDER R. PRUSS

Abstract

Sceptical theism claims that we have vast ignorance about the realm of value and the connections, causal and modal, between goods and bads. This ignorance makes it reasonable for a theist to say that God has reasons beyond our ken for allowing the horrendous evils we observe. But if so, then does this not lead to moral paralysis when we need to prevent evils ourselves? For, for aught that we know, there are reasons beyond our ken for us to allow the evils, and so we should not prevent them. This paralysis argument, however, shall be argued to rest on a confusion between probabilities and expected utilities. A connection between this paralysis argument and Lenman's[1] discussion of the butterfly effect and chaos will be drawn, and the solution offered will apply in both cases.

1 Introduction

Weak sceptical theism (wst) holds that the existence, severity and distribution of observed evils does not noticeably decrease the probability of the existence of God given the massive extent of our ignorance about (a) the realm of value and (b) the connections, causal and modal, between goods and evils. This ignorance, it is claimed, makes it impossible to be confident that a perfect being would have done better to prevent an evil E, say because E might be necessary for some great good beyond our ken. The thesis that the existence, severity and distribution of observed evils do not *at all* decrease the probability of the existence of God because it is no more likely than not that God, if he existed, would on balance have reason to prevent E I will call "strong sceptical theism" (sst).

A presupposition of the discussion is that prior to the consideration of evil, the probability of the existence of God is neither 0 nor 1, and I shall assume this for the sake of the arguments. After all, if the probability of the existence of God is 0 or 1, then it won't be affected—at least in a Bayesian setting—by inductive evidence.

---

[1]   James Lenman, 'Consequentialism and Cluelessness', *Philosophy and Public Affairs* **29** (2000), 342–370.

doi:10.1017/S1358246117000261   ©The Royal Institute of Philosophy and the contributors 2017
Royal Institute of Philosophy Supplement **81** 2017

Alexander R. Pruss

It is important not to overstate either weak or strong sceptical theism. The sceptical theist does not claim to be ignorant in general about what is and is not good or bad, or about ordinary causal and modal connections between goods and bads. She knows that poisoning someone causes death, and that death is something bad. But she denies that the known goods, bads and interconnections are likely to be representative of all of the ones there. For instance, for aught that she knows, while the death of a healthy innocent person is something bad, such a death might be, either in general or in a particular case, a necessary partly constitutive condition for some immense good.

It has been argued that sceptical theism leads to moral paralysis in the case of prevention of evil (e.g., Almeida and Oppy 2003). A standard formulation of this argument is this. Start with the story of Ashley Jones, a twelve-year-old girl raped and bludgeoned to death. We then imagine we could, with no danger to ourselves, have stopped this evil, and then we argue like this:

1. If [strong sceptical theism] is true, then we should be in doubt about whether we should have intervened to prevent Ashley's suffering.
2. We should not be in doubt about whether we should have intervened to prevent Ashley's suffering.
3. So, [strong sceptical theism] is false.[2]

The argument is valid and nobody in the debate denies (2). Thus, the discussion focuses on (1). One response to this influential type of argument is to claim that premises like (1) unduly depend on consequentialist reasoning (for the latest defense of this, see Daniel Howard-Snyder[3]). I shall argue that the extent of consequentialism that is needed for arguments like the above is no greater than the extent to which consequentialism is in fact true, and hence this response is inadequate. Instead, I will argue that the intuitions supporting (1) seem to make the mistake of using probabilities in practical reasoning where expected utilities are needed, and offer a very plausible consequence-focused *prima facie* moral principle that undercuts

---

[2]   Cf. Daniel Howard-Snyder, 'Epistemic Humility, Arguments from Evil, and Moral Skepticism', *Oxford Studies in Philosophy of Religion* 2 (2010), 1–35.
[3]   'Agnosticism, the Moral Skepticism Objection, and Commonsense Morality', in: T. Dougherty and J. P. McBrayer (eds.), *Sceptical Theism: New Essays* (Oxford: Oxford University Press, 2014).

(1). If so, the argument against sceptical theism fails even on the consequentialist grounds on which it was made.

As noticed by Howard-Snyder[4], the debate here parallels the argument in Lenman that the "chaos", or great sensitivity to initial conditions, that we observe in the human world around us undercuts consequentialism. Along the way, I shall draw out this parallel, and my solution will also be a response to Lenman.

Strong sceptical theism is rather implausible. After all, suppose that we observed no evil at all. That would surely be evidence for the existence of God. But it is a Bayesian theorem that if a hypothesis H has a probability that's neither 0 nor 1, and D is evidence for H, then its negation, $\sim D$, is evidence against H. Hence, if the the non-observation of evil is evidence for theism, then the observation of evil is evidence against theism. But it might be quite insignificant evidence for theism, and that is what the sceptical theist probably should say instead of saying that it is no evidence at all. Hence, wst is preferable to sst. However, in responding to the paralysis argument, I will work with sst, since the paralysis argument is more compelling on sst than wst. If my response on behalf of sst is successful, it is even more successful on behalf of wst.

I need to offer an important caveat, however. It has been argued that sceptical theism leads to scepticism *simpliciter* (e.g., Pruss[5]). If so, in particular it leads to scepticism about morality, and hence to moral paralysis. I shall assume for the sake of this paper that the argument that sceptical theism leads to scepticism in general fails, even though I am actually quite sympathetic to that argument.

2 An argument and a fallacy of moral reasoning

Why think that (1) is true? There is an intuitive line of thought:

4.   If sst is true, it is no more likely that preventing Ashley's suffering will lead to an on-balance better outcome than that it will lead to an on-balance worse outcome.

5.   If it is no more likely that preventing Ashley's suffering will lead to an on-balance better outcome than that it will lead to

---

[4]   Op cit. (2010).

[5]   Alexander R. Pruss, 'Sceptical Theism And Plantinga's Evolutionary Argument Against Naturalism' (2010) http://prosblogion.ektopos.com/2010/05/22/sceptical_theism_and_plantingas_evolutionary_argument_against_naturalism.

Alexander R. Pruss

an on-balance worse outcome, consequence-based reasoning does not support preventing Ashley's suffering.

6. If consequence-based reasoning does not support preventing Ashley's suffering, then we should be in doubt whether we should have intervened to prevent Ashley's suffering.

And (1) follows immediately from (4)–(6) by a sequence of hypothetical syllogisms.

Howard-Snyder[6] challenges (6) by opting for a non-consequentialist moral theory. But it is important to note that our moral reasoning requires a significant component of consequence-based reasoning. Suppose two famine-relief organizations serve distant strangers, and the means they employ are morally on par. My decision which organization to give money to should be based precisely on answers to questions about consequences: How many lives can be saved by a donation of that size, how much suffering can be alleviated, and so on? And if an angel were to reveal to me that unbeknownst to me there are unfortunate side-effects of donating to both organizations that cancel out the benefits of the donation, then there would be no point to giving to either.

There will be versions of the Ashley case where (6) is false, say when we have a special relationship with Ashley, such as being a friend or a relative. It may even be the case that when Ashley is a stranger and turns her terrified eyes to us for help, that will constitute such a special relationship.

But suppose Ashley is a distant stranger and the only connection I have with her is that I know that if I press a button, her attacker will be teleported out of her home. Then consequence-based reasoning seems exactly the right kind of reasoning. For suppose I know for sure that the attacker will perpetrate the same heinous act on some other innocent stranger if I teleport him. Then, I argue, I should be at least in doubt whether I should intervene.

For, on the one hand, it could be intrinsically valuable to stand against rape and murder by teleporting the attacker. I would thereby be doing something like 'making a statement', maybe even if no one hears the statement. This provides a reason to teleport the attacker.

On the other hand, there is something deeply morally uncomfortable about deciding by a positive act which of two complete strangers will be raped and murdered. Suppose a trolley is heading for a fork in the track, and the switches are set so it will turn left. There is

[6] Op. cit. (2014).

74

complete stranger lying on the leftward track and another on the rightward track. I could move the switch on the track so the trolley turns right, sparing the stranger on the left, but killing the one on the right. But this seems worse than pointless. Suppose I redirected the trolley to the right, and the mother of the stranger asked me why I killed her daughter. What would I say? 'This was an unintended side-effect of saving the life of the person on the left track.' But the next question could surely be: 'Why was the person on the left track more important to you?' If I said that the person on the left track was *my* daughter, I could imagine being understood. But if I said that they were both equally strangers, the mother's resentment at my meddling could be justified. On the other hand, if I left the trolley alone, I could imagine saying to the mother of the victim on the left track: 'I did nothing, because either way someone would die, and it was not my place to influence who that would be.'

In the case where Ashley is a distant stranger and teleporting the attacker leads to another attack, I started with an intuition that I should teleport the attacker out of Ashley's home. But upon imagining what I would have to say to a parent of the other victim, I lose that intuition.

In any case, it is not my point to argue that in that case I *shouldn't* save Ashley. It is only my point to argue that we should be in doubt when the consequences are balanced and Ashley is a stranger. Thus, when Ashley is a total stranger, (6) is rather plausible. The other premises of the argument for (1), as well as the argument (1)–(3), remain plausible when Ashley is a total stranger. Hence anti-consequentialism is not the way out of the argument.

The problem instead is that (5) is false. It is a fallacious form of consequence-based reasoning.

For suppose there are two deep swimming pools. You know there are ten people drowning in one of the pools, and none in the other. The pools are shrouded in mist and there is a lot of background noise, so you can't tell which pool is which. Suddenly you see a malefactor toss a fair coin, and on the basis of the coin toss decide into which pool to throw a tied-up innocent stranger. Despite the mist, you can see which pool the stranger is being thrown into. You can now press a button that will drain exactly one pool of your choice. (If you try to drain both, everything explodes.) Should you drain the pool with the tied-up stranger (pool *A*) or the one without (pool *B*)?

The probability that pool *A* has more people than pool *B* is 1/2: pool *A* has the tied-up stranger, but that won't make any difference to which pool has more people, since prior to the stranger's being

Alexander R. Pruss

tossed in, there were ten in one pool and none in the other. Likewise, the probability that pool B has more people than pool A is also $1/2$. Thus, the probability that draining pool A produces the better result is $1/2$; this is the same as the probability that draining pool B produces the better result. If an analogue of (5) held in this case, consequence-based reasoning would not support draining pool A.

But consequence-based reasoning clearly does support draining pool A: draining A has a better expectation. This is intuitively true, but can also be checked with an expected value calculation. The expected value of draining pool A is the saving of $1+(1/2)(10) = 6$ lives. The expected value of draining pool B is the saving of $(1/2)(10) = 5$ lives.

The problem with (5) is that consequence-based decisions should not be made on the basis of which action is more likely to be beneficial. They should be made on the basis of something more like an expected utility calculation.

While the pool case will be useful later, thinking about cases of safety checks makes the point even more forcefully. Sally gives tours of the crypt of an old church. At the end of every day, she checks to make sure that no one has been left behind in the crypt when she locks up for the night. It would be quite unpleasant to be locked up in a crypt for the night. Past experience shows her that she finds a person left behind in the crypt once every ten days. It's evening now, and she wants to go home. Sally's son has a minor illness, and she would like to get back to him a few minutes earlier, so she is thinking about skipping the check. She reasons:

> If there is no one in the crypt, going home without checking is better, since it's good for my son that I get home sooner. If there is someone in the crypt, checking is better, since it's terrible to be locked up for the night in the crypt. Since the probability that there is someone in the crypt is only $1/10$, it is much more likely that not checking leads to the better outcome.

But clearly she should check. And while one might reasonably argue for this on the grounds of her special duties to tourists, it remains true that pure consequence reasoning also gives that answer. Being left in a crypt overnight is much more than ten times as bad as having one's mom come home a few minutes later when one is a little sick.

Safety check procedures often violate analogues of (5). It is morally worth making a small effort—even one that imposes small but morally significant costs on others—to prevent an unlikely great bad, even though most likely the better outcome will eventuate if one skips the small effort. In the case of safety checks, one expects that analogues of (5) in fact are quite a serious blight on society. In any instance of a safety check, one can be pretty confident that a better outcome would eventuate from not checking. (Finding problems when doing safety checks surely should be an exception rather than the rule.) But if a safety check is rightly instituted, as it often is, the expected utility of checking is positive.

Of course, a further problem with omitting a safety check is that it leads to a habit of not-checking. However, even if a habit were not being formed, a failure to check simply because the probability of an accident is less than 1/2 would be an egregious breach of responsibility—so egregious, in fact, that even people who omit safety checks typically don't justify their omission by saying that the probability of the check being needed in the given case is less than or equal to 1/2, as an analogue of (5) would have it, but claim that the probability is negligible or something like that (and are sometimes literally fatally wrong about the negligibility).

A specific formulation of a principle like (5) in the literature is given by Almeida and Oppy[7] in their version of the paralysis argument:

> if we do believe that it is not unlikely that there are unknown goods which would justify us in not preventing [an evil] E, then it is very hard to see how we could fail to be justified in not preventing E.

I take it that Almeida and Oppy are committing to this principle:

7.   If it is not unlikely that there are unknown goods which would justify us in not preventing an evil E were the goods known to us, then we are justified in not preventing E.

In an important way this claim is stronger than in (5), since it is easier to meet Almeida and Oppy's 'not unlikely' condition than the probability 1/2 condition in (5). And the swimming pool story is a counterexample to (7), just as it tells against (5). Let E be the evil of the drowning of the innocent person we see thrown into pool A. Further, it is not unlikely—indeed, it has probability 1/2—that there are ten people drowning in swimming pool B. If so, the good of saving their lives would, if known, justify us in not preventing E, since if we knew that there are ten people drowning in pool B,

[7]   Michael J. Almeida and Graham Oppy (2003), 'Sceptical Theism and Evidential Arguments from Evil', *Australasian Journal of Philosophy* **81** (2003) 496–516, 507.

we would drain pool B, not pool A. Hence by (7) we are justified in not draining pool A. But clearly we are obligated to drain pool A.

Just as (5) does, (7) uses probabilities where something more like expected values are needed.

3 Can the mistake be avoided?

We looked at two arguments for the claim that strong sceptical theism implies that, at least on some versions of the story, consequence-based reasoning leads to doubt about whether we should stop Ashley's attacker. Both confused probabilities with expected utilities. The natural question is whether there is some way of avoiding this mistake and still getting to the conclusion along similar lines.

I will argue that the answer is likely negative. Here is the rough intuition. There are known features of the action and unknown ones. The known ones clearly require stopping the attacker, assuming we can do so without undue risk to self or others. The unknown features, were we to know them, would be just as likely to strengthen the case for stopping the attacker as to weaken it, and for any degree by which they could weaken the case for intervention, they could equally well strengthen it to that degree. Thus our information about the unknown features neither favors intervention nor nonintervention. Given that the known features require intervention, and the unknown make no difference given our information, we should still intervene. I will now give a more elaborate version of this argument.

Actions are evaluated on the basis of what I will call 'morally relevant features' or just 'features' for short. These features may include consequences, intentions, relationships, normative statuses of the agent and patient, etc. Consequences include causal consequences, but also constitutive ones—i.e., morally relevant states of affairs partly or wholly constituted by the action and/or its causal consequences. If consequentialism is true, then only consequences are among the 'features'.

An action is required, justified or unjustified *simpliciter* or *on balance* provided that it is required, justified or unjustified (respectively) in the light of all its features. But an action may also be required, justified or unjustified in the light of features of type F. For instance, an action may be justified in light of its consequences, or unjustified in light of its intentions. Whether an action justified or unjustified in light of features of type F is justified *simpliciter* depends on how it fares with respect to features beyond F.

I shall take reasons, as well as requirement, justification or unjustification, to be relative to an agent and her information state. In other words, the interest is in the internalist concepts. For the interest in this paper is whether sceptical theism paralyses an agent morally, and that seems to be an internalist question.

One may have moral reasons for or against an action in light of a feature or a type of feature. I will use 'reason' to mean moral reason. Reasons provided by different features combine and there is, no doubt, some complex relationship between the reasons provided by the features of an action and its requirement and justification statuses. Clearly, if all the features of an action provide reasons for the action, the action is justified, and, very likely, if they all provide reasons against the action, it is unjustified. But how the relationship works in the in-between case, where some features provide reasons in favor of the action and some against, is difficult. Perhaps, for instance, an action is required if and only if on-balance its features provide reason for it.

There is hard work in moral theory to be done in identifying morally relevant features and working out the relationship between requiredness, justification and reasons. But the following is a platitude: reasons—and remember that I am only talking of moral reasons—in favor of an action contribute to its being required and to its being justified while reasons against an action contribute to its being unjustified. This platitude makes this moral principle plausible:

8. Suppose that the features of an action A are divided into two types, X and Y, and suppose that in the light of the features of type X, the action is required (or, respectively, justified) for an agent x, and that features of type Y do not provide x with a reason against A. It defeasibly follows that action A is required (respectively, justified) for x.

The phenomenon of exclusionary reasons requires the defeasibility qualification. Suppose a judge is in a position where recusal is impossible (justice needs to be served, and no other judge is available), but the judge's decision impacts the well-being of the judge's family in such a way that solely in light of the well-being of the judge's family, judicial action A should be taken. Suppose that all the other features of the case mildly support A, but do not require it. Let X be features relevant to the well-being of the judge's family. Let Y be all other features. Among other things, Y will include requirements of procedural justice that require the judge to exclude features of type X from consideration. By itself, Y does not tell against A. But because of these requirements of procedural justice, Y type reasons neutralize the (moral) reason-giving force of X. Consequently, if X were all there was, the judge would be required to do A, but once we throw the reasons of type Y into the mix, even though the Y reasons on their own mildly favor A, the judge is no longer required to do A.

More generally, higher-order reasons affect which first-order reasons count, and how much they count for. In themselves, higher-order reasons in Y may not favor or disfavor an action A, but by affecting how the first-order count they may shift the evaluation for or against A. The possibility of such reasons being found in Y requires the defeasibility qualification in (8).

Now let's go back to Ashley's case. Let X be the facts about what Ashley's sufferings would be like if we do not intervene as well as the other known features of the case. Let Y be all the unknown features. Remember that the reasons we are interested in are internalist reasons in light of the available evidence. We do not have any evidence either way about the unknowns, or so the sceptical theist insists. Given this, the unknowns internalistically favor neither prevention nor non-prevention. On the other hand, X clearly requires us to prevent the crime. So, by (8), we can defeasibly conclude that we should prevent Ashley's sufferings.

The crucial question now is whether sceptical theism provides a defeater. And we need to be clear on what that defeater would be like. The unknown features do not provide an internalist reason against preventing the crime. Depending on what the unknowns actually are, they might provide an externalist reason against prevention, or an additional externalist reason for prevention. However, the defeasibility in (8) comes not from this, but from the possibility of Y containing higher-order reasons that do not themselves favor non-prevention but that exclude some or all the reasons in X.

Higher-order reasons come up in special contexts such as commands, promises, official roles or special relationships. The case of Ashley does not *appear* to be at all like any such context. It may seem odd to rely on this non-appearance, however, in a defense of sceptical theism. After all, the sceptical theist specifically wants to block inferences from the absence of the appearance of a reason to the absence of a reason. But the contexts are different. The sceptical theist's scepticism encompasses the realm of value as well as causal and constitutive connections between localized states of affairs and other morally relevant states of affairs. This scepticism lies at the level of first-order reasons. Here, however, what we are relying on is our ability to know what higher-order reasons there may be. I will argue that we should not have qualms derived from sceptical theist with regard to higher-order reasons in Y when deciding whether to help Ashley.

First, higher-order reasons appear to always be reasons for a particular agent in a particular context. They are reasons for a particular agent to evaluate her first-order reasons in a particular way. That I am commanded by my commander to take yonder hill entirely excludes reasons of personal convenience from my consideration, rather than just outweighing them[8], and hence the command provides *me* with a second-order exclusionary reason. But it does not exclude reasons of my (or your) personal convenience from *your* consideration when you are not subject to that command. In this way, higher-order reasons may well differ from many first-order reasons, since the fact that something is a first-order good for me arguably gives a (defeasible) first-order reason to *every* agent to provide it.

Now, the sceptical theist only professes scepticism about *God's* reasons. In the case of first-order reasons, these may have sufficient overlap with our reasons so as to raise the paralysis problem that we are considering. But scepticism about God's *higher-order* reasons does not with any plausibility lead to scepticism about ours.

Second, we can imagine cases where we don't know about the force of higher-order reasons. These will be rather contrived cases. Let's say you are now in an obvious bit of a difficulty. That gives me reason to help you. But I notice I have amnesia. So for all I know, I promised to leave you to your own devices in a case like this. But the mere chance that I made a promise, with no actual evidence, gives me no reason to refrain from helping. Moreover, just as there is a chance that I promised not to help, there is a chance that I promised to help. The unknown externalist higher-order reasons might readjust the evaluation of the known first-order reasons in favor of not helping but they can also readjust in favor of helping, and so these opposed higher-order unknowns wash out. Thus not knowing whether there might not be a relevant externalist higher-order reason does not defeat the inference in (8).

In summary, by (8), we have a defeasible internalist reason to help Ashley. It looks like the only defeater for (8) is something that would change how reasons combine, and that would have to be a second-order reason. But neither known nor unknown externalist higher-order reasons provide a defeater for the inference.

---

[8] Cf. Joseph Raz, *Practical Reason and Norms*, 2nd ed. (Princeton: Princeton University Press, 1990).

Alexander R. Pruss

Note, too, that the present solution works *better* if consequentialism is true. Higher-order reasons are not a notion consequentialism is particularly friendly to. And when we have only first-order reasons in play, the defeasibility in (8) seems to disappear.

4 The butterfly effect

Sceptical theists are not the only people who have the difficulty that unknown factors morally swamp the known factors. Suppose we take the "butterfly effect" hypothesis from chaos theory really seriously, so that we think relatively small causes, such as a butterfly's wing flutter, can have morally enormous effects down the road, like an earthquake in Japan in ten years.

In his discussion of the butterfly effect, Lenman[9] focuses on identity-involving actions, ones that change who the people populating the earth are. Which of millions of sperm meets up with an ovum is very likely to be different if the timing of intercourse is slightly changed. And it is not hard to change the timing of intercourse. Suppose that Alois Hitler went shopping in the afternoon, and in the evening, together with Klara, conceived Adolf. A small shift in when some other customer entered the store hours earlier could easily have resulted in a shift in when Alois was served, and in turn changed the timing of conception, and brought it about Adolf was never conceived.

Of course, whether Adolf Hitler or—on the positive side—Jonas Salk existed has vast repercussions for the identities of the earth's denizens. But the Hitlers and Salks of the world are not the only ones whose lives have vast repercussions. The same is true for most people—it may just take longer. For a typical person's actions are likely to affect the timing of intercourse for a number of people over a lifetime, not to mention the choices of partners. The extent of the identity-effect will likely then grow exponentially from generation to generation, especially now that our world is so interconnected globally.

And once the identities of much of the earth's population are affected, this will have vast effects on people's wellbeing compared to which the direct effects of our daily actions are likely to pale. What awful dictators will come into existence? Will a great medical researcher who finds a cure for cancer be born in the 22nd century or the 23rd? The wellbeing of millions or even billions depends on this.

[9] Op. cit. (2000).

82

Given plausible assumptions about the chaotic nature of our world, our actions have unpredictable consequences of very large magnitude in the future. That magnitude is likely to be so large that it will completely swamp the predictable short-term consequences.

This leads to a paralysis argument exactly analogous to the one for sceptical theism. Lenman defends this paralysis argument, and Howard-Snyder[10] observes the analogy between the two arguments. The two arguments are indeed analogous, and both are brought down by principle (8). The unknown chaotic consequences can be put into Y, and they neither favor action nor inaction, and so the decision should be made on the basis of the known factors which we can put into X. In fact, the butterfly effect case is easier to handle than the sceptical theism case, because *ex hypothesi* all we are worrying about are consequences, since chaos doesn't provide any mysterious higher-order reasons that might yield a defeater in (8).

5 Weakening the force of reasons

But there is an objection to lines of thought like this. To make the objection clearer, simplify our story by supposing consequentialism is true and that we are deciding between actions A and B. For each action X (where X is A or B), there is a known utility $U_{X,1}$ of consequences and an unknown utility $U_{X,2}$ of consequences, and it is known that the unknown utility swamps the known in the sense that $|U_{A,2} - U_{B,2}| \gg |U_{A,1} - U_{B,1}|$. Moreover, the total utility is just the sum of the two: $U_X = U_{X,1} + U_{X,2}$. Hence if we knew $U_{A,2}$ and $U_{B,2}$, we could make our decision solely on their basis. But we don't. Instead all we know is that $U_{A,1} > U_{B,1}$. And this difference is swamped. How, then, can we decide?

A simplified version of the response that relies on (8) is that we should decide on the basis of the epistemically expected values $E(U_{A,1} + U_{A,2})$ and $E(U_{B,1} + U_{B,2})$. Since $U_{A,1}$ and $U_{B,1}$ are simply known—let's say they are known to be equal to some numbers α and β—these two values respectively come to: $\alpha + E(U_{A,2})$ and $\beta + E(U_{B,2})$. But now in the complete absence of information about the unknown effects, we have no way to distinguish $U_{A,2}$ and $U_{B,2}$ epistemically, and hence it seems reasonable to say $E(U_{A,2}) = E(U_{B,2})$ as we are dealing with epistemic expectations. Since we

10   Op. cit. (2010).

Alexander R. Pruss

know that $\alpha > \beta$, we then have $E(U_{A,1}+U_{A,2}) > E(U_{B,1}+U_{B,2})$, and we should do A. There is no paralysis.

So far so good. But now Lenman[11] raises this worry. Given that the difference between α and β is much smaller than the difference between $U_{A,2}$ and $U_{B,2}$, the force of the reason to do A instead of B is pretty small. We are deciding something that has enormous repercussions on the basis of something very minor. Lenman[12] offers the analogy about deciding between two possible landing locations for the Allies on the continent, and in the absence of any data as to which is better, deciding on the basis of the wellbeing of a particular dog known to be at one of these locations.

One answer is that the defeasible conclusion in (8) can be strengthened. If the Y features don't provide a reason against A, then the strength of the reason for A overall is no less than that provided by the X features. But while this is very plausible, it does not address the intuitions behind Lenman's worry.

The dog case is probably easy to handle. It is insulting to the soldiers to make the decision on the basis of the life of a dog. But vary the case so it's not insulting. Suppose that somehow (due to a prophecy?) we know that a landing at A will cost 100,000 lives and a landing at B will cost 100,001 lives. If all who would die on A would also die on B, and if we know who that 100,001st victim on B would be, say Jim, we clearly ought to go for a landing on A. And the strength of the reason for landing on A is exactly the strength of the reason for saving Jim's life. The fact that 100,000 people are going to die at Jim's side does nothing to weaken the value of Jim's life.

But what if we don't know who the extra survivor on landing A is, and we keep everything the same? This, too, should make no difference. The value of that anonymous (that is, anonymous to us: but a mother, brother, sister, friend, daughter, etc. to those close to him or her) extra survivor is no less for the hundred thousand dying at his or her side. Recall the swimming pool case. The sense in which we knew who the extra person is was very thin: we saw a particular stranger in the distance, but we didn't know him or her from Adam, as we say.

Finally, suppose that the identities of those who would die on either landing are completely different. In case A, 100,000 people—anonymous to us—will die. In case B, 100,001 will. Is there a significant difference in the strength of reasons to land on A? Without being able to identify particular individuals across the

[11] Op. cit. 356–358.
[12] Op. cit. 357.

two scenarios, it may be difficult to *feel* the difference. But let's switch cases. Alice is about to unleash 100,000 doses of a poison gas, where each dose will kill a random person in New York. Her friend Bob can't stop her, but thinks to himself: 'There is not much difference between 100,000 anonymous people and 100,001. If I load another dose in the canister, probably quite a different collection of hundred thousand people will die.' And he adds a dose.

Alice is a murderer a hundred thousand times over. But Bob's action is morally on par with murder, too. It is no less on par with murder for the fact that the identities of the victims were likely switched as a result of his action. But even though Bob is effectively a murderer, there may not be a person whom he murdered, since the dose Bob added presumably got mixed with all the others, and contributed a little to the deaths of many. (The law will get Bob for conspiracy to murder, but that is just a pragmatic solution.)

Still, even if we can only call Bob's action 'on par with murder' and not really a 'murder', he is no less bad than a murderer. To make the point perhaps clearer, suppose that 100,000 people each with malice contribute one dose of poison gas to the canister. Each is as bad as if they had released that dose in some place where it wasn't mixed with other doses but killed one individual.[13]

We can make the same point on the side of saving lives. Carl is about to release an antidote to a poison that was set to kill a million people. Unfortunately, Carl only has 100,000 doses of the antidote, so he is going to save only 100,000 lives. Dale comes by with an extra dose. Dale's action is morally on par with saving one more life, even if the identities changed.

How hard should we fight to keep Bob from adding his dose of poison gas to Alice's canister? Exactly as hard as we would to prevent one random murder. How hard should Dale try to come up with that extra dose? As hard as it would be worth trying to save one life. We can, after all, imagine 100,000 people each working hard to contribute a dose of antidote. They should each work as hard as one should to save one life. The strength of a reason isn't measured by feeling, but by how hard it makes it rational to follow the reason—what cost the reason makes it rational to accept.

And by the same token, the reason to land on landing A instead of B, when one fewer soldier will die, is as strong as the reason to save a life. It doesn't *feel* as strong. But the mistake here is a non-financial version of the well-known mistake by which someone will drive

---

[13]   Cf. the cases in Derek Parfit, *Reasons and Persons*, Oxford: Oxford University Press, 1987), chapter 3.

across town to get a free $5 bottle of shampoo but who would not bother to cross the street to a different dealership to buy a car for $5 less. The apparent decreases in the strength of reasons in light of the butterfly effect or sceptical theist hypotheses are a kind of moral illusion, akin to this financial illusion.

6 Conclusions

The paralysis argument against sceptical theism confuses reasoning about which action is more likely to result in the better outcome with reasoning about which action is a better bet. Resolving this confusion does not require going beyond consequence-based reasoning, but also does not require committing to consequence-based reasoning. I offer a defeasible moral principle, (8), that suggests that whether consequentialism is true or not, it is very unlikely that there is a way of repairing the paralysis argument. This also solves the related, but not specifically theistic, problem of alleged paralysis coming from the butterfly effect. Sceptical theism and chaos may be problematic, but not for reasons of paralysis.

Baylor University
alexander_pruss@baylor.edu

Detachment, Rationality and Evidence: Towards a More Humane Religious Epistemology

JOHN COTTINGHAM

Abstract

Some truths cannot be accessed 'cold', from a detached and impersonal standpoint, but require personal commitment and even moral change in order for the relevant evidence to come to light. The truths of religion may be of this kind. Moreover, recent work in psychology and neurophysiology suggests that our knowledge of the world comes in different forms, the detached critical scrutiny associated with 'the left-brain' and the more intuitive and holistic awareness mediated by the 'right brain'. Much contemporary philosophy privileges the former kind of knowledge, but in areas such as religion this may be a mistake.[1]

1. Outlooks, pictures, frameworks, lenses

How to people come to religious belief? There are no doubt many different ways of coming to believe something. The most common is an almost instantaneous process, as when you believe there is a chair in the corner of the room, or that your cup of coffee has gone cold. Such ordinary basic beliefs are formed pretty much involuntarily when you look round the room, or take a sip of coffee. In this kind of belief-formation process, the mind seems almost passive: the data from the senses are processed by the brain, and the belief spontaneously forms itself in the mind, 'just like that'. There is the chair; the coffee is cold. End of story.

Very different from this is the case where there is a more active contribution from the agent, as when someone examines the evidence for a proposition before reaching a decision on what to believe. For example, she sees spots of water on the window pane, opens the window and holds her hand out, and after a moment or two's waiting, decides that the rain has now stopped.

[1]   A version of this paper was delivered at a conference on Religious Epistemology held at Heythrop College, University of London, in June 2015. I am grateful to the organizer, Stephen Law, and to participants for helpful discussion. The paper draws extensively on material from my *How to Believe* (London: Bloomsbury, 2015).

doi:10.1017/S1358246117000236   ©The Royal Institute of Philosophy and the contributors 2017
Royal Institute of Philosophy Supplement **81** 2017

John Cottingham

Both these ways of believing are familiar enough, and conceivably a person might come to religious belief in one of these two relatively straightforward ways, or something analogous to them. But I suspect that what characteristically and typically turns someone into a religious believer is an altogether different kind of process, more radical in terms of the psychological changes undergone, and more comprehensive and all-pervasive in its scope and extent. People sometimes speak of contrasting 'visions' of the world, and one thinks here of what philosophers call a 'worldview' or a 'picture of reality'. In the German language, always more comfortable with compound nouns than English, it is common to speak of an individual or a society having a *Weltanschauung,* literally a 'world-outlook'. The German term has had a variety of meanings since it was first coined in the late eighteenth century by Kant (albeit in a rather special sense),[2] but has been widely adopted into English as an accepted way of referring to a general system of ideas or a comprehensive system of thought.

Although a system of thought is a complicated structure which may have many ramifications, it can often have at its centre a certain simple and vivid picture of the way things are. Sometimes such a picture may take hold of us almost without our being aware of it, as Ludwig Wittgenstein points out when he speaks of a picture 'holding us captive'.[3] The context of that particular remark was a discussion of how the structure of language can predispose us to think in a certain way, and indeed mislead us, or 'bewitch the intelligence,' as he puts it elsewhere.[4] But other pictures may be more benign, as when Wittgenstein speaks of a religious outlook as involving the feeling of absolute safety: 'nothing can injure me, whatever happens'. This sort of attitude, Wittgenstein went on to say, is obviously different from a feeling of safely about some ordinary matter such as feeling secure that you can't get whooping cough because you've had it once already. To ordinary common sense ways of thinking, you might well be safe from whooping cough, but there are obviously other diseases you could get, so to say you are safe 'whatever happens' is in a literal sense nonsense. But this should not lead us to dismiss such language out of hand, since it is inevitable that thinking about religion

---

[2] By Immanuel Kant, *Critique of Judgement* [*Kritik der Urteilskraft,* 1790], Part I, Bk 2, §26.

[3] Ludwig Wittgenstein, *Philosophical Investigations* [*Philosophische Untersuchungen,* 1953], transl. G. E. M. Anscombe (New York: Macmillan, 1958), §115.

[4] Wittgenstein, *Philosophical Investigations,* §109.

will sooner or later 'run up against the boundaries of language'. Such religious thinking, according to Wittgenstein, springs from a tendency in the human mind that demands 'deep respect', as he put it, even though it might not add to our factual knowledge.[5]

Despite such expressions of sympathy for religious ways of thinking, Wittgenstein was himself unable to embrace any traditional religious world picture, although he continued to wrestle with what was involved in adopting a religious outlook. In one of the places where he discusses religious belief he speaks of it as involving commitment 'to a set of co-ordinates'. A variant reading has the more general phrase 'a system of reference' (*einem Bezugssystem*).[6] One of the thoughts underlying this comparison may be that a system of reference, or a system of measurement (for example the metric system), is something that is adopted even though it cannot itself be verified in the way that a given measurement within the system ('this stick is three meters long') can be verified. The metric system does not itself belong in the complete set of true propositions expressing metric measurements; rather it is a *framework* that generates the possibility of such measurements. So Wittgenstein may be suggesting that a religious outlook or belief-system does not refer to objects or items within the world but instead provides a general framework for understanding and interpreting it.

But not all frameworks are equally congenial to everyone. If we pursue the metric analogy, it is clear that there are some anti-Europeans in early twenty-first century Great Britain who deplore the adoption of the metric system, and greatly prefer more 'human' measurements like the foot and the yard, originally based on traditional ways of pacing out distances. Whether or not we sympathise with this, there is no contradiction, in this type of debate, in someone saying 'you stick to your system and I'll stick to mine'. Neither system is 'the right one' in any fundamental sense; nor are they really in conflict (though of course people may be anxious for political or cultural reasons to champion one over the other).

What is at stake in the measurement example is thus not truth, but convenience or utility or pleasingness, or something of that sort. But in the religious case, when people give their allegiance to a given framework or picture of reality such as theism, they do so because they believe it to be *true*. Perhaps, in so far as it may shape our

---

[5] Wittgenstein, 'A Lecture on Ethics' [1929], *Philosophical Review* (1965), 8.

[6] Wittgenstein, manuscript of 1947, in *Culture and Value* (Oxford: Blackwell, 1998), 73.

John Cottingham

thoughts and actions, it can be compared to a 'system of co-ordinates'; but for the believer this is not just a matter of convenience or personal preference. It is taken by the believer to be a system that genuinely reflects the structure of reality, uncovers the true purpose and meaning of human existence, and serves as a valid and trustworthy guide to how we should live our lives. And this in turn raises the question of how we can decide whether the theistic picture of reality is true? How we can know whether to accept it and put it at the centre of our outlook on the world?

The religious sceptic will already have answered this epistemic question by saying we *can't* know, and will go on to say that in the absence of any compelling evidence there can be no reason to consider accepting it. One has to admit that there is a certain robust reasonableness about this, calling to mind the definition of a sceptic (best uttered in a dry and slightly ironic tone) as 'one who prefers his statements to be true'. If we dramatize the process of assessing a picture of reality and imagine the religious worldview as a picture in the literal sense, like a painting hung in a gallery, the sceptic can be thought of as one who stands back, scrutinizes it carefully, raises a doubtful eyebrow, shakes his head and calmly walks on.

The simile does not quite work, however. For if we accept the idea that a worldview functions as a 'framework of interpretation', then it will hardly be comparable to a particular painting hung in a gallery alongside others. On reflection it is clear that a framework of interpretation could not be the kind of thing that can be assessed in the way a single item in a collection can be assessed, since it is not an 'item' or 'object' at all. If we have to find a simile for the kind of thing it is, we might say it is more like a *lens*: not an item in the collection but that which enables us to see the collection in the first place, or to bring it into proper focus so as to grasp its significance.

Unfortunately though, the 'lens' model is not quite satisfactory either, or at least it raises further difficulties of its own. Taken one way, it might suggest an implanted lens in the eye, like a pair of spectacles which it is impossible to take off. One thinks here of Immanuel Kant's theory that our human experience of the world is necessarily structured in terms of notions like space and time and causality, so that we cannot but process the world around us in these terms, and experience it accordingly.[7] But using this kind of lens analogy for a

---

[7]   Immanuel Kant, *Prolegomena to any Future Metaphysic that will be able to present itself as a Science* [*Prolegomena zu einer jeden künftigen Metaphysik die als Wissenschaft wird auftreten können,* 1783], ed. G. Zöller and P. Lucas (Oxford: Oxford University Press, 2004), Part II; cf. Adrian

religious worldview would imply that we necessarily *have* to view or interpret the world in a certain way, the way suggested by a religious perspective. Yet it is obvious that this is not so. Many people start off with a religious outlook, perhaps inherited from parents and teachers, and then come to discard it (just as, conversely, there are cases of agnostics or atheists who change from a neutral or anti-religious to a religious worldview). So there is nothing necessary or unavoidable about understanding or experiencing the world in a religious way.

We therefore need a better model for what a religious world picture is like, a model that presents it not as a pair of spectacles that cannot be taken off, nor on the other hand as an object or item in the gallery that is simply there in front of us to be scrutinized and evaluated. We need to find room for the idea that a religious worldview can be adopted or rejected, but we also need to do justice to the thought that such adoption or rejection is not a 'flat' process of detached inspection and assessment, but something more dynamic, something that engages us at a deeper level of involvement.

2. Transformation and truth

The examples I began with, seeing an coffee cup on the table, or deciding if it is raining, tend to imply a fairly straightforward conception in which the world which has such and such features – and that in the light of how those features present themselves to us we have to decide how to conduct ourselves towards it. But humans are not just passive observers of the world; we constantly interact with it. That much is true even of non-human animals. Yet in our human case there is an additional aspect, a kind of creative dimension. Instead of merely processing the data from the five senses in ways determined by the innate structure of our sense organs and nervous systems and shaped by our previous perceptions, humans have additional faculties, active creative powers of reflecting on and interpreting their experience. A group of children exploring a garden will not simply map it out and find their way round, but will, even from a very young age, transform it creatively into a rich locus of imaginative play, places to hide, scary dark corners to avoid, bushes that are 'monsters' to be confronted, banks that are places of safety and refuge.

Moore, *The Evolution of Metaphysics* (Cambridge: Cambridge University Press, 2012), 120.

John Cottingham

The sober rationalist may dismiss this as 'mere imagination', or may take a more functional approach, talking of play as a useful mechanism which affords practice in learning to deal with what will later be the practical hazards of adult life. But far more is involved than that. In virtue of our unique conceptual powers and sensibilities, all of us do much more than encounter the world; we transform it, creating out of the raw data of perception a whole rich 'lifeworld', a world full of meaning and value. In other words, in our basic relation to the world there is, in the human case, a kind of *poetry*, in the strict etymological sense of *poēsis*, a 'making'. What the Nobel Laureate Seamus Heaney discusses in the following passage in reference to his own literary activity as a poet applies in a wider sense to the entire transformative relation in which human beings stand to the world:

> In order that human beings bring about the most radiant conditions for themselves to inhabit, it is essential that the vision of reality which poetry offers should be transformative, more than just a printout of the given circumstances of its time and place. The poet who would be most the poet has to attempt an act of writing that outstrips the conditions even as it observes them.[8]

Because we often think of imaginative writing as 'fiction', it is easy to misunderstand the point being made here as the banal claim that human beings have the capacity to 'make things up'. Much literary output is indeed fictional, in the sense that it does not record historical occurrences or consist of literal factual propositions. But Heaney's point about human beings bringing about the 'most radiant conditions for themselves to inhabit' is a much more subtle and important one than that. Part of what he is saying is that the writer never produces a mere 'printout of given circumstances'. Indeed, on reflection it is clear that we cannot really grasp what such a raw 'printout' would be: there can never be, for humans, an uninterpreted world, a world that is not always already a world of significance, a world where some features are salient because of what they mean for us, and the way they point beyond themselves to other elements of our lifeworld.

The key concept at work here is not 'fiction' in the sense of making up things that are literally false, but *transformation*. When Heaney says that poetry should have a 'transformative' function, he does not mean that it distorts or alters things, changing a given item into

---

[8] Seamus Heaney, 'Joy or Night', in *Finders Keepers: Selected Prose 1971–2001* (London: Faber, 2002).

92

something else. What the poet deals with, as the passage makes clear, is the real world: he has a 'vision of *reality*'. It is a vision that sharply embraces and delineates what is there in view, disclosing its significance. Poetry is thus not fiction, but *truth*, truth in the sense Martin Heidegger famously referred to when he harked back to the etymology of the Greek word for truth, *alētheia*, literally an 'uncon-cealment' (in German *Unverborgenheit*), a disclosing of what is (partly) hidden.[9]

Thinking more about Heaney's idea of a 'transformative vision', we can see that it has application far beyond the literary domain. When humans interpret the world, as they necessarily must, what happens is a kind of co-operation between the reality that is there before them and their own attempt at understanding it. And that is never a final and completed process; by its nature it engages the restlessness of the human search for meaning. So again when Heaney talks of the poet's writing 'outstripping the conditions even as it observes them', we can see something of the elusive mystery of Being. The nature of reality is never finally packaged up and definitively presented to us, and we always reach beyond the given in our human struggle to understand it.

The restlessness and the struggle that are inevitably involved here again mark a contrast between us and the other animals. For them, the world is 'given' in a relatively determined and fixed way; they are not confronted with a mystery of being, because they are simply wholly absorbed in dealing with it in ways directly related to their immediate needs. In this sense, they are 'at home' in the world, in a manner we can never be – a point powerfully underlined by Rilke in his *Duino Elegies*:

> *und die findigen Tiere merken es schon,*
> *das wir nicht sehr verläßlich zu Haus sind*
> *in der gedeuteten Welt.*

> and the resourceful beasts notice quite soon
> that we are not very securely at home
> in the interpreted world.[10]

Once we have got this far, it is possible to see that a purely science-based understanding of the world can never be a neutral way of

---

[9]   Martin Heidegger, *Being and Time* [*Sein und Zeit,* 1927], transl. J. Macquarrie and E. Robinson (New York: Harper and Row, 1962), §219.

[10]   Rainer Maria Rilke, *Duino Elegies* [*Duineser Elegien,* 1923], First Elegy (transl. JC).

John Cottingham

describing what is 'given'. Rather it is one particular way of dealing with reality – a way that involves a deliberate decision to filter out the interpreted world of meaning and value in favour of certain structural and quantitative descriptions that are suitable for the purposes of explanation and prediction. This is not at all to disparage science, whose achievements have been enormous. But at the very least it opens the way for the possibility of alternative visions of reality, which cannot be dismissed as mere 'flights of imagination' or 'fiction', but which have a right to be considered as potential disclosures of the meaning of the world we inhabit. Theistic belief, belief in a personal Being who is the ultimate ground underlying the mystery of being in the universe and the source of its meaning and value, is just such a vision, a transformative vision that brings into salience features of the world which simply drop out of view in the quantitative printouts of particle interactions, or (to take another example) in the Buddhist style conception of reality as an impersonal flow of conditions that arise and pass away, leaving our own deepest individuality and selfhood as nothing more than an illusion.

3. The double helix

The process of coming to accept a certain vision of reality is not only transformative in the sense of changing what is seen, or disclosing what was not seen before. It is also transformative in the sense that it changes the *experiencing subject*, altering the way in which he or she is able to see things. In other words, the transformation involved when a religious worldview is adopted is a *dual transformation*: not only does a whole new reality come into view, not only is the world, as it were, transfigured, but the subject who experiences that world is also made new. One might say, following the famous image of William Blake, that the 'doors of perception' are cleansed.[11] And this is not just an epistemic change, a change in our ability of discern or know certain things, but it is also a *moral* change, a change in the character and dispositions of the perceiver – indeed the two types of change are inextricably linked.

It follows that such a process, unlike the more routine types of belief formation discussed earlier, is a highly dynamic one. Unlike the involuntary mechanisms which automatically generate my belief that there is table in front of me when I open my eyes, or the 'flat' process of deciding what to believe, when I dispassionately

[11]   William Blake, *The Marriage of Heaven and Hell* [1790].

evaluate the evidence and come to a conclusion, I am instead caught up in an *complex upward spiral of change*, an *interactive double helix*, if you will, where the world starts to look different, and simultaneously my character, as I confront the world, starts to undergo a radical shift.

Now it might seem that this leads to a vicious circle, or, to put it another way, that I could never gain any entry point into the upward spiral in the first place. If I have to undergo interior change in order accept a certain worldview, or in order to begin to discern something of what it discloses, how will such necessary interior change be possible at an earlier stage, before the transformed vision or the world has already begun to work on me? Perhaps I already have to be a certain kind of person in order for the vision to be available, or in order such a vision to take a grip on my imagination; while conversely, if I am not such a person, then the vision could never take hold of me in the first place. If this is right, it begins to look as if the world is going to be divided into two groups of people, those whose lives are imbued and informed with a certain picture of reality, or who are perhaps, in Wittgenstein's phrase, 'held captive' by it, and those who are outside the charmed (or deluded) circle, and have no way of breaking into it.

On this kind of account of the difference between believers and non-believers, there is nothing much that either group can do to change. To put the matter in the way some theologians have understood it, there will be the 'saved', already predisposed and pre-destined to believe and accept the true worldview, and the 'damned' whose 'hearts are hardened', and who could never come to believe.[12] How then can anyone break into the 'upward spiral' of belief? The answer given by those who take a strict 'predestinarian' line is that no one can, unless they are already divinely so predisposed. On this view, salvation cannot be earned, and religious belief cannot be attained by any voluntary process of evaluating the evidence or scrutinizing the facts, or indeed any other human voluntary activity, but can only come as a free unmerited gift, by divine grace.

For present purposes however, we can pursue our reflections on the psychology of belief-formation without being drawn into such theological niceties. The metaphor of the 'upward spiral' or 'double helix', introduced a moment ago, suggests that the adoption of a belief system or a worldview is not a matter of simply coming up against a religious belief system and then straightforwardly assenting to it or rejecting it. Rather, it may involve successive stages of transformation, both in the subject and in the way the relevant picture of

---

[12]   Cf. John Calvin, *Institutes* [*Christianae religionis institutio,* 1536].

reality takes shape. To make this clearer, let me go back to the 'picture gallery' metaphor I was using earlier, but this time consider not one of the paintings hung on the wall, but a prism, fashioned of stained glass and suspended from a cord high up in middle of the room. Many visitors ignore it or give it a wide berth, hurrying past to inspect the individual paintings. But others, without perhaps quite knowing why, linger and find themselves moving near it or standing under it. Once the resistance to moving in that direction has been set aside, the room begins, from this position, to look different. Patterns of light and colour in the air and on the walls become visible and begin to glow and shine, in turn bringing about changes in the attitude of the subject. She ceases to be a detached spectator, bent on inspecting and assessing the various objects in the gallery, and starts to be *moved*: responsive feelings of delight and awe begin to surface. And now she begins to be enthralled, as from this vantage point all manner of objects in the room are illuminated by the prism, bring into focus complex new relationships, which begin to form a wondrous pattern. The meaning of the whole exhibition, before occluded, now comes vividly into view.

Without labouring the simile, which like all similes cannot be pushed too far, it may at least indicate a possible way out of the impasse described earlier – the problem of there being no way to break into the 'upward spiral' of belief. What begins as a mere minimal willingness to pause and look around, becomes, as the transformations take affect, an attentive looking, and then a delighted looking; and at each stage, richer dimensions of reality come into focus. As we progress up the spiral of committed attention, we ourselves undergo interior change, and this leads to changes in perception, awareness of new relationships, which in their turn generate further transformations, both in the reality that is presented to me, and in how I perceive its meaning.

4. A new model of religious understanding

One of the implications of what I've been saying is that we need a *new model of religious understanding*.[13] Now the phrase 'religious understanding' is open to various interpretations, but I propose we

---

[13]   This final section of the paper draws on material from my 'Transcending science: humane models of religious understanding', in F. Ellis (ed.), New Models of Religious Understanding (Oxford: Oxford University Press, 2017), pp. 23–41.

construe it in what I take to be the most intuitively obvious way, namely adverbially, as it were, as referring to a certain *mode* or *manner* of understanding the world. In similar fashion we speak, for example, of 'scientific understanding', of 'musical understanding', or of 'psychoanalytic understanding'; and in all these domains we mean a characteristic way of relating to or interpreting reality, or some part of it. The question about religious understanding then becomes *what is it to relate to the world religiously?* or *what is it to understand things in a religious way?*

Let me pursue the analogy with *musical understanding.* By this phrase someone might perhaps have in mind the kind of theoretical intellectual understanding that musicologists aim at – for example being able to expound the difference between 'just intonation' (where the ratios of notes are related by small whole numbers) and 'equal temperament' (where all notes are defined as multiples of the same basic interval). But in contrast to this kind of abstract or theoretical approach, one might be thinking instead of the kind of rich cognitive and emotional awareness that we attribute to someone when we say, in ordinary parlance, that he or she is a 'very musical' person. These two different kinds of musical understanding seem logically, psychologically and causally quite distinct. It seems possible, for instance, that someone could score very well in a musicological examination where the candidates are required to write an essay on equal temperament, or some similar topic, while not having much, if any, musical understanding in the latter sense of having a rich musical sensibility; and conversely, it seems clear that someone could be gifted with outstanding intuitive musical awareness without any grasp of theory (an actual example is the opera singer Njabulo Madlala, who at the age of nineteen auditioned at the Guildhall and was offered a full scholarship even though, as he subsequently informed the adjudicators, he had had no musical education and could not even read music).[14]

The basic thought here is that one can have a kind of direct, intuitive, way of understanding something that needs to be distinguished from a detached, analytic way of approaching it. Iain McGilchrist, in his groundbreaking book *The Master and His Emissary,* draws on recent brain science concerning the different functions of the two hemispheres of the brain. And he speaks of

> two ways of being in the world, both of which are essential. One is to allow things to be present to us in all their embodied

---

[14] See *Financial Times* 17 October 2014, http://www.ft.com/cms/s/0/9474020c-54c2-11e4-bac2-00144feab7de.html#axzz3HAHgd3MI

particularity, with all their changeability and impermanence and their interconnectedness, as part of a whole which is forever in flux. In this world we, too, feel connected to what we experience, part of that whole, not confined in subjective isolation from a world that is viewed as objective. The other is to step outside the flow of experience and 'experience' our experience in a special way: to re-present the world in a form that is less truthful, but apparently clearer, and therefore cast in a form which is more useful for manipulation of the world and one another. This world is explicitly abstracted, compartmentalised, fragmented ... essentially lifeless. From this world we feel detached, but in relation to it we are powerful.[15]

The kind of 'power' McGilchrist refers to here is very seductive for philosophers. We like to feel we are detached scrutineers, above the fray, mapping out the logical structure of various theories and pronouncing our lordly judgements about their viability. But if McGilchrist is right, there is a danger in always allowing the logical, analytic, detached mode of awareness [the 'left-brain' skills, if you will] to predominate in our philosophical thinking. Similarly, Eleonore Stump has recently deplored analytic philosophy's tendency to 'suppose that left-brain skills alone will reveal to us all that is philosophically interesting about the world'.[16]

The key point here is that much moral and religious discourse is *multilayered* – it carries a rich charge of symbolic significance that resonates with us on many different levels of understanding, not all of them fully grasped by the reflective, analytic mind. Any plausible account of the human condition must make space for the crucial role of imaginative, symbolic, and poetic forms of understanding in deepening our awareness of ourselves and the reality we inhabit. This in turn suggests it's a serious error to try to reduce the religious outlook to a bald set of factual assertions whose literal propositional content is then to be clinically isolated and assessed.[17] Perhaps the kind of connection the religious outlook searches for cannot be achieved by the critical scrutiny of the intellect alone, but requires a process of attunement, or *Stimmung,* to use a Heideggerian

[15]   Iain McGilchrist, *The Master and His Emissary* (New Haven: Yale University Press, 2009), 93 (slightly adapted).
[16]   Eleonore Stump, *Wandering in Darkness* (Oxford: Oxford University Press, 2010), 24–25.
[17]   See John Cottingham, *Philosophy of Religion: Towards a More Humane Approach* (Cambridge: Cambridge University Press, 2014).

term,[18] a moral and spiritual opening of the self to the presence of the divine.

One implication of this (with which I will close) is that we need a new epistemology for thinking about religious belief and its basis. Both the Dawkins-type critics of religion, and (interestingly) many mainstream natural theologians as well, operate with an *epistemology of control*. We stand back, scrutinize the evidence, retaining our power and autonomy in a 'left-brain' kind of way, and pronounce on the existence or otherwise of God. But why assume that the divine presence will detectable via intellectual analysis of formal arguments or observational data? The ancient Judaeo-Christian idea of the *Deus absconditus* (the 'hidden God') suggests a deity who is less interested in proving his existence or demonstrating his power than in the moral conversion and freely given love of his creatures, and in guiding aright the steps of those who 'seek him with all their heart', in Pascal's phrase.[19] And when we think about the means of such conversion, it becomes clear that it could never operate through detached intellectual argument alone, or through the dispassionate evaluation of 'spectator evidence', to use Paul Moser's label.[20] Hence those who insist on casting the 'God question' in a form that is apt for evaluation by 'left brain skills' alone may be missing the core issue that is at stake in the adoption of a religious worldview. The question is not 'Can I, while scrutinizing the data and remaining detached and fully in control, satisfy myself of the rational acceptability of belief in God?'; but rather something like the following: 'How can I embark on a path of moral and spiritual change which might open me to a deeper awareness of something that I now glimpse only faintly.'

In short, this is an area where we need to relinquish the epistemology of control, and substitute an *epistemology of receptivity*. This is not special pleading on behalf of religion, since there are all sorts of other areas of life – appreciation of poetry, of music, entering into any kind of personal relationship, where we need to be 'porous', to use Martha Nussbaum's term: not hard, detached, critical evaluators, but open, yielding, receptive listeners.[21] Otherwise, while we pride

---

[18] See Heidegger, *Being and Time*, H 137. See also George Steiner, *Heidegger* (London: Fontana, 2nd edn, 1992), 55.
[19] Blaise Pascal, Pascal, *Pensées* [1670], ed. L. Lafuma (Paris: Seuil, 1962), no. 427.
[20] Paul Moser, *The Elusive God: Reorienting Religious Epistemology* (Cambridge: Cambridge University Press, 2008), 47.
[21] Martha Nussbaum, *Love's Knowledge* (Oxford: Oxford University Press, 1990), 282.

John Cottingham

ourselves of being in control and evaluating the evidence, *we will actually be closing ourselves off from allowing the evidence to become manifest to us*.

So this is what I mean by moving towards a 'more humane' religious epistemology. Instead of being fixated on scientific models, and on impersonal, spectator evidence, we should be prepared to allow that there are many areas of human life, including the domain of religion, but by no means confined to this, where we have to give up the fantasy of being lofty, detached evaluators, surveying the data and pronouncing our verdict. Whether we like it or not, we have to be involved, to be receptive. This does not mean being gullible, or blindly accepting the first idea that comes into our minds. But it does mean that we have to be prepared to listen, to be porous, to be permeable, to allow the possibility that there are parts of reality that have a transformative effect on us, and that, if we allow ourselves to be transformed, we may be taken to new levels of awareness and understanding. The analogies I've mentioned, with literary awareness, with poetic awareness, with musical awareness, and with personal awareness, with our intimate relations with others, may sound alarm bells for those who want to keep knowledge clinical, detached, and scientific. But being human involves being open to all aspects of reality, and adopting an epistemology that allows for this may be a way for us all, philosophers of religion included, to become more fully human.

Reading University, Professorial Research
Fellow at Heythrop College, London
jgcottingham@mac.com

Faith and Reason

DUNCAN PRITCHARD

Abstract

A novel account of the rationality of religious belief is offered, called *quasi-fideism*. According to this proposal, we are neither to think of religious belief as completely immune to rational evaluation nor are we to deny that it involves fundamental commitments which are arational. Moreover, a parity argument is presented to the effect that religious belief is no different from ordinary rational belief in presupposing such fundamental arational commitments. This proposal is shown to be rooted in Wittgenstein's remarks on hinge commitments in *On Certainty*, remarks which it is claimed were in turn influenced by John Henry Newman's treatment of the rationality of religious belief in *An Essay in Aid of a Grammar of Assent*.

> '*The difficulty is to realize the groundlessness of our believing.*'
> Wittgenstein, *On Certainty* [*OC*], §166

> '*None of us can think or act without the acceptance of truths, not intuitive, not demonstrated, yet sovereign.*'
> John Henry Newman, *An Essay in Aid of a Grammar of Assent*
> [*EAGE*], 150

1. The Rationality of Religious Belief

To what extent can religious belief be rational? Answers to this question have tended to cluster around two extremes. On the one hand, there is *epistemic heroism*. This is the stance that a perfectly sound epistemic basis can be offered for religious belief - one that is epistemic through-and-through -and hence that there is no standing problem to the idea that such beliefs can be rationally held. In its most radical form, epistemic heroism involves arguing that there are *a priori* proofs of the existence of the God, or at least that there are *a priori* considerations which demonstrate that His existence is highly likely (or more likely than not at any rate).[1] But epistemic heroism doesn't need to be quite so extreme. A more modest line of

---

[1]   See, for example, Richard Swinburne *The Existence of God*, (Oxford: Oxford University Press, 1979).

doi:10.1017/S135824611700025X   © The Royal Institute of Philosophy and the contributors 2017

argument—found in important work by *reformed epistemologists* like Alvin Plantinga[2], for example—makes no appeal to *a priori* proofs, but merely skilfully demonstrates that a plausible general epistemology, at least if applied in a consistent way to religious belief (i.e., such that there are no 'double-standards' in play), can deliver the required positive epistemic result.

There are a number of difficulties that afflict epistemic heroism, but perhaps the most pressing is that it doesn't seem altogether true to the nature of religious conviction. Religious conviction, after all, is at its most fundamental level a matter of *faith* rather than reason. Indeed, there would something seriously amiss with someone who professed to a faith in God, but who was nonetheless willing to abandon this commitment once faced with counterevidence that she is unable to rationally dismiss (e.g., the problem of evil). If she did abandon her faith as soon as it is challenged in this way, we would rather say that she never had the faith that she professed to have in the first place. And yet giving up one's commitments in light of the presentation of counterevidence that one cannot rationally dismiss is one of the hallmarks of the rational person. It follows that if we take the nature of religious commitment seriously, then we should be suspicious of accounts of the rationality of religious belief that are epistemic through-and-through.

But if we don't head in the heroic direction, then what is the alternative? The standard line is that unless epistemic heroism can be made to work, then we will need to acquiesce with *epistemic capitulation*. Here I have primarily in mind the kind of *fideistic* accounts of the nature of religious belief which effectively remove such belief from being rationally assessable at all. The fideist will maintain that to rationally evaluate religious belief, as if it were akin to other kinds of belief (e.g., perceptual belief), is somehow to misunderstand its nature. Unlike epistemic heroism, views which espouse what I am calling epistemic capitulation, such as fideism, take the nature of religious commitment, and in particular the fact that faith rather than reason lies at the heart of that commitment, very seriously. Unfortunately, they also effectively epistemically 'ghettoize' religious belief. Not only is there no through-and-through epistemic basis offered for religious belief, there is no epistemic basis at all, in contrast to other forms of belief.

---

[2]   Alvin Plantinga, 'Reason and Belief in God', *Faith and Rationality*, (ed.) A. Plantinga & N. Wolterstorff, (Notre Dame, Indiana: University of Notre Dame Press, 1983), 16–93 and also Plantinga's *Warranted Christian Belief* (New York: Oxford University Press, 2000).

Is there not a way to steer between these two extremes? I think so. I maintain that there is a way of thinking about the rationality of religious belief which simultaneously takes seriously the fact that such belief is, at root, a matter of faith rather than reason while also avoiding the trap of treating religious belief as being such that it should be epistemically evaluated completely differently from ordinary belief. I call such a view *quasi-fideism*.

Although the defensibility of such a proposal is obviously independent of whoever proposed it, such a position can be found in the work of John Henry Newman, particularly his master work, *An Essay in Aid of a Grammar of Assent* [EAGE]. Significantly, this proposal is also arguably found in the final notebooks of Wittgenstein (published as *On Certainty* [OC][3]), which I think were highly influenced by an engagement with Newman's work. Newman's writings on the epistemology of religious belief are these days largely ignored (by analytical philosophers at any rate), and his influence on Wittgenstein's final notebooks is barely registered in the literature. Worse, Wittgenstein's treatment of the epistemology of religious belief is standardly construed as a straightforward fideistic position, and hence the subtleties of his actual position in this regard are overlooked. A proper understanding of quasi-fideism, and its historical sources, thus goes some way towards rectifying these intellectual injustices.

2. Wittgenstein on the Structure of Rational Evaluation

Reformed epistemologists standardly motivate their position by offering what is known as a *parity argument*.[4] This is the idea that when we consistently apply the epistemic standards in play as regards ordinary belief, we find that religious belief is no worse off. So, for example, one version of a parity argument states that when we epistemically evaluate religious belief in the same way that we epistemically evaluate perceptual belief, then the former turns out

---

[3]   *On Certainty*, (eds.) G. E. M. Anscombe & G. H. von Wright, (tr.) D. Paul & G. E. M. Anscombe, (Blackwell, Oxford, 1969).

[4]   See especially William Alston's 'Religious Experience and Religious Belief', *Noûs* **16** (1982), 3–12, 'Is Religious Belief Rational?', *The Life of Religion*, (ed.) S. M. Harrison & R. C. Taylor, (Lanham Maryland: University Press of America, 1986), 1–15, and *Perceiving God: The Epistemology of Religious Experience*, (Cornell, Ithaca: Cornell University Press, 1991).

to be of just the same epistemic standing as the latter. Assuming this claim is correct, it is dialectically significant because, radical scepticism aside, there isn't thought to be a standing challenge to the epistemic standing of perceptual belief. Hence, given that scepticism about the rationality of religious belief is meant to be specific to religious belief (i.e., and not a trivial consequence of radical scepticism more generally), then it follows that there is not a serious epistemic challenge to religious belief.

As we will see, quasi-fideism also involves a kind of parity argument, albeit of a very different sort. Whereas standard parity arguments aim to show that religious belief can be just as rational as another kind of belief which is generally considered to be through-and-through rational, quasi-fideism takes a more radical line. According to the quasi-fideist, our everyday beliefs that we take to be through-and-through rational in fact presuppose fundamental arational commitments—i.e., commitments which are not rationally grounded. This is where the parity argument comes in, since the proponent of quasi-fideism claims that although it is true that religious belief presupposes fundamental arational commitments, this is not a basis for a specific scepticism about the rationality of religious belief since *all* belief, even beliefs which we generally hold to be paradigmatically rational, also presuppose fundamental arational commitments. Put another way, while the quasi-fideist grants that religious belief is, at root, a matter of faith rather than reason, she nonetheless holds that this doesn't disqualify religious belief from being rational since all belief is, at root, a matter of faith rather than reason.

One can find a development of this kind of position in Wittgenstein's last notebooks, subsequently published as *On Certainty*. In this work, Wittgenstein is grappling with the idea that our most basic commitments—i.e., commitments which express propositions about which we are optimally certain—are in their nature rationally groundless. Part of the stimulus for this investigation are the kinds of everyday certainties famously enumerated by G. E. Moore[5] (1925; 1939), which are these days known as *Moorean certainties*. These include propositions such as that one has two hands, that one has never been to the moon, that one is speaking English, and so on. Moore believed that the special certainty that

[5]   G.E. Moore, (1925). 'A Defence of Common Sense', *Contemporary British Philosophy* (2nd series), (ed.) J. H. Muirhead, (London: Allen and Unwin, 1925) and 'Proof of an External World', *Proceedings of the British Academy* **25** (1939) 273–300.

we attach to these propositions provides them with a special epistemic status that enables them to play a kind of foundational role in our epistemic practices. Wittgenstein took a very different view. He argues instead that we can make no sense of the idea that we can rationally evaluate that which we are most certain of, where this includes both a *negative* rational evaluation (i.e., a rational doubt of these commitments) or a *positive* rational evaluation (i.e., offer rational support for these commitments).

Consider the Moorean certainty that (for most people, and in normal circumstances), one has two hands. Wittgenstein writes:

> My having two hands is, in normal circumstances, as certain as anything that I could produce in evidence for it.
>
> That is why I am not in a position to take the sight of my hand as evidence for it. (OC, §250)

Here Wittgenstein is suggesting that to conceive of this proposition as rationally grounded is to suppose that the rational grounds are more certain than the proposition itself, which of course is *ex hypothesi* impossible since it is held to be optimally certain. Wittgenstein brings this point into sharp relief by highlighting how odd it would be for one to treat one's conviction that one has two hands as being grounded in one's sight of one's hand. Consider this passage:

> If a blind man were to ask me 'Have you got two hands?' I should not make sure by looking. If I were to have any doubt of it, then I don't know why I should trust my eyes. For why shouldn't I test my *eyes* by looking to find out whether I see my two hands? *What* is to be tested by *what*? (OC, §125)

In normal circumstances, one doesn't need to check by looking that one has two hands—indeed, imagine how odd it would be if someone were to do this—and moreover to check by looking would make no sense anyway. If one doubts that one has two hands, then one ought not to believe what one's eyesight tells one, since this is no more certain than that one has two hands, which is in doubt.

The point is that these basic certainties, precisely in virtue of being basic certainties, are thereby immune to rational evaluation, whether positive or negative. Moreover, Wittgenstein is quite clear that this is not an incidental fact about our rational practices, but rather reflects an important truth about the very nature of rational evaluations. This is that it is a prerequisite of being a rational subject at all—i.e., one who can undertake rational evaluations and have rational beliefs—that one has such basic arational certainties. To attempt to rationally evaluate a Moorean certainty is thus an attempt to do something impossible. It constitutes a failure to appreciate an important fact about the very nature of rational evaluation, which is that all rational evaluation presupposed arational commitments.

Wittgenstein repeatedly urges that the very idea of rationally doubting a Moorean certainty is incoherent. Such a doubt, he writes, would 'drag everything with it and plunge it into chaos.' (OC, §613) Doubt of a Moorean certainty is deemed akin to doubting everything, but Wittgenstein cautions that:

> If you tried to doubt everything you would not get as far as doubting anything. The game of doubting itself presupposes certainty. (OC, §115)

And elsewhere, 'A doubt that doubted everything would not be a doubt' (OC, §450; cf. OC, §§370; 490; 613). What goes here for doubt also applies to rational belief, for Wittgenstein would equally argue that the game of rational believing also presupposes Moorean certainties. All rational evaluation, whether positive or negative, presupposes arational commitments.

Wittgenstein famously characterise these arational certainties in terms of the metaphor of a hinge. Consider this famous passage:

> [...] the *questions* that we raise and our *doubts* depend upon the fact that some propositions are exempt from doubt, are as it were like hinges on which those turn.
> That is to say, it belongs to the logic of our scientific investigations that certain things are *in deed* not doubted.
> But it isn't that the situation is like this: We just *can't* investigate everything, and for that reason we are forced to rest content with assumption. If I want the door to turn, the hinges must stay put. (OC, §§341–3)[6]

Wittgenstein is thus offering a radical new conception of the structure of rational evaluation, one that has arational hinge commitments at its heart. In particular, he is arguing that both the sceptical project of offering a wholesale negative rational evaluation of our beliefs and the traditional anti-sceptical (e.g., Moorean) project of offering a

[6] Although the 'hinge' metaphor is the dominant symbolism in the book, it is accompanied by various other metaphors, such as the following: that these propositions constitute the 'scaffolding' of our thoughts (OC, §211); that they form the 'foundations of our language-games' (OC, §§401–3); and also that they represent the implicit 'world-picture' from within which we inquire, the 'inherited background against which [*we*] distinguish between true and false' (OC, §§94–5).

wholesale positive rational evaluation of our beliefs are simply incoherent. This is because the very idea of a wholesale rational evaluation
is itself incoherent, for it is in the very nature of rational evaluations
that they take place relative to hinge commitments which are both
groundless and indubitable.[7]

A comment about Wittgenstein's use of the hinge metaphor will be
helpful here. What Wittgenstein intended with this metaphor is the
idea that these commitments need to stand fast in order for rational
evaluations to be possible, just as hinges on a door need to stand
fast in order for the door to turn. One aspect of the metaphor that
has mislead some commentators, however, is the fact that hinges on
a door are usually *moveable*—that is, one can shift them about the
door and thereby enable the door to turn in different ways. This
has led some commentators to treat one's hinge commitments as at
least sometimes optional, in that one can acquire or lose them at
will (e.g., by changing the nature of one's investigation).[8] I think it
is reasonably clear from a close reading of Wittgenstein's remarks
on hinge commitments, however, that he does not regard them as optional in this way. Instead, he regards such commitments as being of a
visceral nature, as 'animal' (OC, §359), and as involving a kind of
'primitive' trust (OC, §475). Indeed, Wittgenstein is adamant that
these commitments are not only completely unresponsive to rational

---

[7]   Note that it is more common in the literature to refer to *hinge proposi-*
tions rather than *hinge commitments*. The reason why I have departed from
standard practice in this regard is that what is important about these basic
commitments is precisely the nature of the commitment itself (i.e., the out-
right certainty that one is expressing) rather than the proposition that is
being committed to. Indeed, I think that a focus on the latter has tended
to obscure the point that Wittgenstein was trying to make in this regard.

[8]   See, for example, M. Williams, *Unnatural Doubts: Epistemological*
Realism and the Basis of Scepticism, (Oxford: Blackwell, 1991) on 'methodo-
logical necessities' (which can be lost by simply changing one's disciplinary
inquiry), and C. Wright, 'Warrant for Nothing (and Foundations for
Free)?', *Proceedings of the Aristotelian Society* **78** (supp. vol.) (2004),
167–212 on 'entitlements of cognitive project' (which essentially involve
opting to trust certain claims that are essential to a particular cognitive
project). See Duncan Pritchard 'Unnatural Doubts', *Skeptical Solutions:*
Provocations of Philosophy, (eds.) G. A. Bruno *&* A. Rutherford, (Oxford:
Oxford University Press, forthcoming) for detailed discussion of the
former proposal, and also Pritchard, 'Entitlement and the Groundlessness
of Our Believing', *Contemporary Perspectives on Scepticism and Perceptual*
Justification, (eds.) D. Dodd *&* E. Zardini (Oxford: Oxford University
Press, 2014) 190–213 for detailed discussion of the latter proposal.

Duncan Pritchard

considerations, but are also not acquired via rational processes. They are instead 'swallowed down' (OC, §143) as part of a picture of the world that accompanies, and underpins, the specific things that one is taught (e.g., OC, §§152–53).

I think that once we take this aspect of Wittgenstein's account of hinge commitments seriously, then it follows that we shouldn't think of these commitments as beliefs at all, at least where by 'belief' we have in mind the kind of propositional attitude that epistemologists are concerned with (i.e., the sort of propositional attitude which is a constituent of rationally grounded knowledge).[9] This is because belief in this sense does have a basic level of responsiveness to rational considerations, in that it is a propositional attitude which is by its nature truth-directed.[10] This doesn't mean that one can't have irrational beliefs, of course, since manifestly one can. But it does mean that there is a conceptual incoherence in the idea that one has a belief that is completely unresponsive to rational considerations.

Imagine, for example, a parent who regards their child as innocent of charges brought against her even though it becomes clear that there is absolutely no reason for thinking that this is the case (e.g., the evidence for her guilt is overwhelming, and she is unable to offer any evidence in her defence). At some point, as the weight of the evidence becomes apparent, we would no longer classify her propositional attitude of one of belief but rather as something else (e.g., a wishful thinking or a hope). The same applies to our hinge commitments. Once we recognise that they are completely unresponsive to rational considerations—to the extent that one would retain such commitments even while recognising that one had no rational basis for regarding them as true—then they cease to be plausible candidates for being beliefs.

I think that appreciating this point about hinge commitments helps us to evade a problem that has afflicted attempts to develop a fully-fledged hinge epistemology—i.e., an epistemology that takes seriously the idea that all rational evaluation presupposes arational

---

[9] There are, of course, many notions of belief operative in the philosophical literature. See L. Stevenson, 'Six Levels of Mentality', *Philosophical Explorations* **5**, (2002), 105–24 for a survey of some key kinds of belief.

[10] Just to be clear: henceforth I will be talking of belief in the specific sense of that propositional attitude which is a component part of rationally grounded knowledge.

hinge commitments. Nearly all epistemologists would endorse the following principle:

Closure Principle for Rationally Grounded Knowledge
If S has rationally grounded knowledge that p, and S competently deduces from p that q, thereby forming a belief that q on this basis while retaining her rationally grounded knowledge that p, then S has rationally grounded knowledge that q.

What is so compelling about this principle is that competent deduction is a paradigm instance of a rational process. Accordingly, if one acquires a belief from one's rationally grounded knowledge via competent deduction, then how could that belief fail to be itself an instance of rationally grounded knowledge?[11]

The problem, however, is that it can look like this principle is in conflict with the idea that we have hinge commitments, at least insofar as the groundless nature of these hinge commitments is meant to be compatible with one's other beliefs being in the market for rationally grounded knowledge (which they had better be, if the view is not to collapse into radical scepticism). This is because on the face of it one could employ this principle to competently deduce, and thereby come to have rationally grounded knowledge of, one of one's hinge commitments that is entailed by a proposition that one has rationally grounded knowledge of. Conversely, if this isn't possible, then it seems that one is committed to regarding the antecedent belief in this entailment as not being an instance of rationally grounded knowledge after all.

---

[11] Note that epistemologists have denied a closely related—but ultimately very different—principle, which is the general idea that knowledge is closed under known entailments. See, for example, F. Dretske, 'Epistemic Operators', *Journal of Philosophy* **67** (1970), 1007–23 and R. Nozick, *Philosophical Explanations* (Oxford: Oxford University Press, 1981). Crucially, denying that knowledge is closed under known entailments is quite compatible with the endorsement of the closure-style principle just articulated. C. Wright (e.g., 'Warrant for Nothing (and Foundations for Free)?', *Proceedings of the Aristotelian Society* **78** (supp. vol.) (2004), 167–212) has also motivated, on Wittgensteinian grounds, the denial of a principle more in the vicinity of the principle under discussion, though I think this relates to a mistaken understanding of Wittgenstein's notion of hinge commitments, as I explain in my 'Entitlement and the Groundlessness of Our Believing', *Contemporary Perspectives on Scepticism and Perceptual Justification*, (eds.) D. Dodd & E. Zardini (Oxford: Oxford University Press, 2014) 190–213.

Wittgenstein seemed to be aware of this problem. Consider this passage:

> 'It is certain that after the battle of Austerlitz Napoleon … Well, in that case it's surely also certain that the earth existed then.' (OC, §183)

The point is that our commitment to the idea that the earth didn't just pop into existence in recent history (just after one was born, for example) looks like a hinge commitment that one holds. And yet what Napoleon did after the battle of Austerlitz looks like an ordinary historical claim that one can have rationally grounded knowledge of (e.g., by consulting historical documents). Hence with the closure principle articulated above in play, it seems that one could competently deduce the hinge claim from one's rationally grounded knowledge of the non-hinge claim, and thereby come to have rationally grounded knowledge of it. Conversely, if that isn't possible—as proponents of a hinge epistemology are compelled to maintain—then wouldn't that show that one doesn't have rationally grounded knowledge of the non-hinge claim after all? One can see how this line of argument can potentially threaten the idea that hinge commitments are consistent with rationally held belief.

Once we recognise that our hinge commitments are not beliefs, however—and, relatedly, not the kind of propositional attitudes that can be acquired via rational processes, like competent deduction—then we can resolve this problem. The nub of the matter is that what makes the closure principle so compelling is that it involves the acquisition of a *belief* via a paradigm case of a *rational process*. It is only with these claims in play that the principle seems unassailable. But if one's hinge commitments are by their nature never beliefs and never acquired via rational processes, then it follows that they simply cannot be plugged into closure-style inferences in the manner that we have been supposing. It follows that a proponent of a hinge epistemology can consistently endorse the closure principle set out above as there is no essential conflict between these two theses. In particular, it is entirely compatible with the closure principle that, in line with a hinge epistemology, one can simultaneously have rationally grounded knowledge of non-hinge beliefs while lacking rationally grounded knowledge of one's hinge commitments.

Some further remarks about the nature of Wittgenstein's account of hinge commitments are in order. On the face of it, it can look as if our hinge commitments form a heterogeneous class, since they don't obviously have much in common (aside from the fact that they are regarded as certainties). Moreover, they can also look very relative to person, place, epoch and culture. That I've never been to the moon, for example, may be a hinge commitment for both Moore's generation and ours, but one can easily imagine a future generation which doesn't treat this as a hinge commitment. These features of our hinge commitments can make them look rather mysterious items in our epistemic architecture.

This variability in one's specific hinge commitments is, however, superficial, and masks the underlying core that is common to all of these commitments. For what all our hinge commitments express is our basic certainty that we are not radically and fundamentally in error. Call this our *über hinge commitment*. It is this commitment that Wittgenstein thinks needs to be in place in order for one to be a rational subject who undertakes rational evaluations. Our other, more specific, hinge commitments—that one has two hands, that one has never been to the moon, etc.,—are merely expressions of our basic über hinge commitment. That is, one expresses one's general über hinge commitment by manifesting one's commitment to specific propositions which, if one were wrong about, would call into question the über hinge commitment. By characterising our hinge commitments in this fashion, I think we end up with a way of making sense of a number of their features.

First, notice that the claim that one cannot rationally evaluate one's hinge commitments because much clearer once we reflect that to do such a thing is in effect to attempt a rational evaluation of one's über hinge commitment. For the idea that there is some deep incoherence in attempting the rationally evaluate one's über hinge commitment looks very plausible indeed. How could one possibly undertake a rational evaluation of whether one is radically and fundamentally mistaken? Relatedly, the idea that this commitment is non-optional for rational subjects is also compelling.

Second, thinking of our hinge commitments in this way can also explain how they might change over time, and how they can apparently be so variable from person to person. Which specific propositions will codify one's über hinge commitment will inevitably depend on one's beliefs as a whole, so as they change so might one's specific hinge commitments. For example, if one lives long enough to be alive during an age when space travel is so common that one could well have been to the moon without realising it, then inevitably it will now no longer be one of one's hinge commitments that one has never been to the moon. Viewed this way, there is nothing remotely mysterious about this shift in one's hinge commitments.

Third, one might be tempted to think that any proposition about which one is optimally certain thereby qualifies as a hinge commitment. But I think that this would be a mistake. It would obviously be undesirable to treat pathological cases of certainty as thereby hinge commitments, for example. On the account of hinge commitments under consideration, however, we have a principled basis for differentiating genuine hinge commitments from merely optimal certainties, since only the former codify one's über hinge commitment. Waking up one morning and finding oneself convinced that there are fairies at the end of one's garden will not cut the mustard on this score, as given one's wider set of beliefs this is clearly something that one could be wrong about without calling into question the über hinge commitment.

Finally, fourth, this way of thinking about the nature of hinge commitments also lessens the concern that such a view might lead to epistemic relativism. One can see the general shape of the worry, in that if our hinge commitments really are such an heterogeneous and highly variable class, then what is to stop the development of bodies of people with radically different hinge commitments? The problem is that these people would embrace epistemic systems which were epistemically incommensurable with one another, in that there would be no rational way of resolving disagreements. But is it possible for there to be such divergence in one's basic hinge commitments?

For one thing, notice that the über hinge commitment will be a constant in this regard. Remember too that these basic certainties are often about relatively mundane propositions, and hence typically concern essentially shared subject matters. For example, someone growing up China may well have the hinge commitment that they live in China, while someone growing up in England might have the hinge commitment that they live in England. But is this really a divergence in their hinge commitments? In effect, don't they both share a common hinge commitment regarding the country where they live? My point is that when hinge commitments are properly understood, the scope for radical divergence in one's hinge commitments starts to look implausible. Indeed, if anything, I think we should expect there to be large overlaps in hinge commitments, of a kind that should militate against the possibility of a widespread epistemic incommensurability. As Wittgenstein puts the issue at one point, in order to be a rational subject at all, one 'must already judge in conformity with mankind.' (OC, §156)[12,13]

3. Faith and Reason

We are now in a position to see how a hinge epistemology might lead to a quasi-fideistic view about the rationality of religious belief. What is particularly interesting in this context is that there is quite a lot of evidence that Wittgenstein's remarks on hinge commitments were heavily influenced by the work of John Henry Newman, and in particular his defence of the rationality of religious belief in *An Essay in Aid of a Grammar of Assent*. In this work Newman opposes a Lockean conception of our basis for religious belief. Locke famously argued in

---

[12] I explore the topic of epistemic relativism in more detail in Pritchard 'Epistemic Relativism, Epistemic Incommensurability and Wittgensteinian Epistemology', *Blackwell Companion to Relativism*, (ed.) S. Hales, (Oxford: Blackwell, 2010) 266–85. See also Pritchard, 'Defusing Epistemic Relativism', *Synthese* **169** (2009) 397–412. For more on this topic as it arises in *On Certainty*, see M. Williams, 'Why (Wittgensteinian) Contextualism is not Relativism', *Episteme* 4 (2007), 93–114 and A. Coliva *Moore and Wittgenstein: Scepticism, Certainty, and Common Sense* (London: Palgrave Macmillan, 2010).

[13] It should be stressed that the account offered here of hinge commitments is not universally shared; indeed, there are several competing accounts of this notion available in the literature, though it would obviously take me too far afield to describe them in detail here. For some of the key defences of competing proposals, see M. McGinn, M. *Sense and Certainty: A Dissolution of Scepticism* (Oxford: Blackwell, 1989), M. Williams, *Unnatural Doubts: Epistemological Realism and the Basis of Scepticism* (Oxford: Blackwell, 1991), D. Moyal-Sharrock, D., *Understanding Wittgenstein's On Certainty* (London: Palgrave Macmillan, 2004). A. Coliva, *Moore and Wittgenstein: Scepticism, Certainty, and Common Sense* (London: Palgrave Macmillan, 2010), A. Coliva, *Extended Rationality: A Hinge Epistemology* (London: Palgrave Macmillan, 2015), and G. Schönbaumsfeld, *The Illusion of Doubt* (Oxford: Oxford University Press, forthcoming). For two surveys of this literature, see D. Pritchard 'Wittgenstein on Scepticism', *Oxford Handbook on Wittgenstein*, (eds.) O. Kuusela & M. McGinn (Oxford: Oxford University Press, 2011) 521–47. I further develop my own reading of Wittgenstein's epistemology in Pritchard 'Wittgenstein and the Groundlessness of Our Believing', *Synthese* 189 (2012) 255–72 and *Epistemic Angst: Radical Skepticism and the Groundlessness of Our Believing* (Princeton, NJ: Princeton University Press, 2015).

his *Essay Concerning Human Understanding* that reason must be our last judge and guide in everything.'[14] Accordingly, he maintained that religious beliefs should be put before the tribunal of reason just like any other. In particular, he argued that strength of belief should be a function of the strength of epistemic support such a belief enjoys, such that beyond a high enough level of strength this support can license certainty. In this Locke was opposing those religious believers he called the 'enthusiasts', who believe what they do 'because it is a revelation, and have no other reason for its being a revelation but because they are fully persuaded, without any other reason, that it is true, they believe it to be a revelation only because they strongly believe it to be a revelation; which is a very unsafe ground to proceed on, either in our tenets or actions.'[15]

While Locke is concerned only to demarcate rational religious belief from irrational religious belief, the standards he applies are apt to result in a general scepticism about the rationality of religious belief, particularly once one notes that (absent an *a priori* basis for religious belief anyway), religious belief is often grounded in reasons which can at least on the face of it appear little better than that offered in support of the enthusiasts' religious belief. Does the religious believer possess any solid independent basis for holding her beliefs (i.e., a basis which doesn't already presuppose the general truth of her religious worldview)? If not, then it is hard to see how it would pass the Lockean test.

In contrast to this Lockean view about rational belief, Newman argues that many of the propositions about which we are most certain do not enjoy anything like the kind of epistemic support that Locke imagines. The list of propositions he cites in this regard is very interesting:

We are sure beyond all hazard of a mistake that our own self is not the only being existing; that there is an external world; that it is a system with parts and a whole, a universe carried on by laws; and that the future is affected by the past. We accept and hold with an unqualified assent, that the earth, considered as a phenomenon, is a globe; that all its regions see the sun by turns; that there are vast tracts on it of land and water; that there are really existing cities on definite sites, which go by the names of London, Paris, Florence, and Madrid. We are sure that Paris or London, unless suddenly swallowed by an earthquake or burned to the ground, is today just what it was yesterday, when we left it. We laugh to scorn the idea that we had no parents though we have

---

[14] See Locke (1979 [1689], IV, xix, p. 14).
[15] See Locke (1979 [1689], IV, xix, p. 11).

no memory of our birth; that we shall never depart this life, though we can have no experience of the future. (EAGE, 149)[16]

Note that the propositions are all empirical certainties of the general Moorean kind that we saw that Wittgenstein was concerned with above. Indeed, the example that everyone has parents is explicitly considered by Wittgenstein in this regard on several occasions in *On Certainty* (OC, §§211, 239, 282, 335). Newman's point is that for all these cases we lack any epistemic basis which is commensurate with the level of certainty involved; *a fortiori*, we lack the kind of epistemic basis that Locke would demand for reasonable belief in this regard. Indeed, suppose we applied the test that we applied to religious belief above and asked whether one has an independent basis for beliefs such as this—i.e., a basis which does not already presuppose that one's general conception of the world is correct. Would these beliefs pass this test? Surely not. And yet all these beliefs seem eminently reasonable. In fact, they seem to be paradigm cases of what counts as ordinary reasonable belief.

Newman is thus offering the kind of parity argument in defence of the rationality of religious belief that we noted above. Lockean epistemology effectively raises the bar for rational religious belief by requiring a rational basis which is commensurate with the level of conviction involved. This is presented as part of a general view about rational belief and conviction, and hence on the face of it does not fall foul of a parity argument. But if we grant that Newman is right that normal rational belief can involve complete conviction even while lacking a corresponding rational status, then it follows that a double-standard is being applied to religious belief in this regard after all. For why should religious belief be subject to epistemic censure when cases of rational non-religious conviction which exhibit the very same epistemic properties are treated as paradigmatically rational? Put another way, if the Lockean line were consistently applied, then it would be in danger of undermining the epistemic legitimacy of everyday beliefs as well as religious beliefs. There is thus no principled route from the Lockean conception of reasonable belief to a scepticism which is specifically focussed on religious belief.

Newman's way of defending religious belief is thus by showing how the epistemic standing of ordinary belief is very different from how we might suppose it to be, such that it is ultimately not fundamentally different from religious belief. On the Lockean picture of

---

[16] A further example which Newman discusses at length is our conviction that Great Britain is an island (EAGE, 234ff).

rational belief, one's conviction in a particular proposition could be no stronger than the rational support one has in favour of it, and yet this picture of rational belief is manifestly (argues Newman) in conflict with our ordinary conception of rational belief, on which paradigmatically rational beliefs which are regarded as optimally certain possess very little rational support (and certainly nothing by way of independent rational support).[17]

In terms of Newman's own terminology, it is what he calls 'simple assent', which is the kind of conviction we have in these everyday truths, that lies at the heart of our system of rational beliefs, in contrast to the reason-based certainty that Locke thought should be playing this role. Moreover, like Wittgenstein, Newman held that such simple assent is already presupposed in our practices of offering reasons for and against particular propositions. As Wolfgang Kienzler puts the point, according to Newman:

> [B]efore we acquire the capacity to doubt, we already have a set of very firm beliefs that we did not gain by way of reflection but through our upbringing or just through everyday life.[18]

This should remind us of Wittgenstein's claim that one's hinge commitments are not explicitly taught to us, but rather comprise that

[17]   Newman offers an intriguing take on Hume's treatment of belief in miracles which is salient here. Very roughly, Hume claimed that given the nature of miracles *qua* extraordinary events (and given also some further claims, such as certain facts about human psychology), it follows that it would be more rational to doubt the testimonial evidence offered for miracles than it would be to accept that a miracle had occurred on this testimonial basis. While accepting the general principles in play in Hume's argument, Newman nonetheless contends that in a particular case it can be rational to accept the existence of a miracle on a testimonial basis. For what matters is the specific way in which this commitment to the occurrence of a miracle fits within the religious worldview of the agent, with its attendant hinge commitments. Indeed, Newman goes so far as to suggest that one's commitment to the occurrence of the miracle could be a matter of simple assent, in which case one is not to think of the testimony as providing a rational basis for the belief in a miracle at all. To this extent Newman's stance is potentially logically compatible with Hume's, in that Hume was targeting beliefs in miracles which are epistemically grounded in testimony—i.e., and not simply the causal product of testimony—whereas for Newman it seems the beliefs in question need not be grounded in this way at all. See EAGE (243 *&* ff.). For a recent overview of the literature regarding Hume's stance on miracles, see Pritchard *&* Richmond (2012).

[18]   W. Kienzler, 'Wittgenstein and John Henry Newman On Certainty', *Grazer Philosophische Studien* **71** (2006), 117–138.

which we 'swallow down' along with everything we are explicitly taught.

The commonalities between Newman's approach to rational belief and Wittgenstein's approach to this subject in *On Certainty* are no accident. There is a lot of historical evidence to suggest that Wittgenstein read Newman's work very carefully and was inspired by it.[19] With this evidence in mind, it ought to be clear that the basic idea behind the localised conception of rational support put forward by Wittgenstein, such that our practices of giving reasons always presuppose arational hinge commitments which are not themselves subject to rational evaluation, is already present in Newman's work. Where Moore's work connects with Newman's ideas is in his focus on everyday certainties. Wittgenstein's critique of Moore is, however, a Newman-inspired critique: while these Moorean certainties do play a foundational role in our rational practices, this is precisely not because they have a special positive rational status. Indeed, the point is rather that their foundational role entails that they cannot be the kind of commitment which is rationally grounded.

Seeing Wittgenstein's treatment of hinge commitments through the lens of Newman's account of the rationality of religious belief *An Essay in Aid of a Grammar of Assent* helps us to understand why a Wittgensteinian treatment of the rationality of religious belief should be cast along quasi-fideistic lines (rather than fideistic lines, which is how it is ordinarily understood).[20] The crux of the

---

[19]   Although a number of commentators note Newman's influence on Wittgenstein in his later work - such as A. Kenny, (1990). 'Newman as a Philosopher of Religion', *Newman: A Man For Our Time*, (ed.) D. Brown (London: Morehouse Press, 1990) 98–122, A. Kenny 'John Henry Newman on the Justification of Faith', in his *What is Faith? Essays in the Philosophy of Religion* (Oxford: Oxford University Press, 1992), and C. Barrett, 'Newman and Wittgenstein on the Rationality of Religious Belief', *Newman and Conversion*, (ed.) I. Ker, (Notre Dame, Indiana: Notre Dame University Press, 1997) 89–99 - for a thorough account of how their thinking is related, along with a comprehensive discussion of the historical evidence to back up this claim, see Kienzler op. cit. In particular, Kienzler offers a compelling case for treating Wittgenstein's reference to 'Newman' in *On Certainty* (OC, §1) as referring to John Henry Newman (and not to a different 'Newman' entirely, such as the scholar Max Newman, a contemporary of Wittgenstein's at Cambridge).

[20]   For some key discussions of Wittgensteinian fideism, see K. Nielsen, K. 'Wittgensteinian Fideism', *Philosophy* **42** (1967) 237–54 and D.Z. Phillips, *Religion Without Explanation* (Oxford: Oxford University Press, 1976). To be fair, it should be emphasised that those authors which attribute

Duncan Pritchard

matter is that the basic religious convictions of one who has faith will form part of that person's hinge commitments, and hence will be part of the bedrock against which rational evaluations are undertaken. In this way, some of the person's religious beliefs will be rationally held, and hence in the market for being rationally grounded knowledge, even though such beliefs presuppose essentially arational hinge commitments. In this respect, however, religious belief is not fundamentally different from ordinary rational belief, since the latter also presupposes essentially arational hinge commitments. The religious believer's overall set of commitments thus includes fundamental commitments which are more a matter of faith than of reason, but this fact alone doesn't mark any epistemically significant difference between the life of faith and a life lived without it. With the relationship between faith and reason and its role in the production of rational belief understood along quasi-fideistic lines, religious commitment can be at its most fundamental level a matter of faith and yet there nonetheless be rational religious beliefs.[21,22]

UC Irvine and University of Edinburgh
dhpritch@uci.edu

---

a straightforward fideism to Wittgenstein often don't have his remarks on hinge commitments in *On Certainty* in mind, but rather comments he makes about the rationality of religious belief elsewhere, particularly L. Wittgenstein, *Wittgenstein's Lectures and Conversations on Aesthetics, Psychology and Religious Belief*, (ed.) C. Barrett (Oxford: Basil Blackwell, 1966).

[21] For further discussion of quasi-fideism, and of the relationship between Wittgenstein's remarks on hinge commitments and Newman's religious epistemology, see D. Pritchard, 'Wittgensteinian Quasi-Fideism', *Oxford Studies in the Philosophy of Religion* 4 (2011), 145–59 and 'Wittgenstein on Faith and Reason: The Influence of Newman', *God, Truth and Other Enigmas*, (ed.) M. Szatkowski, (Berlin: Walter de Gruyter, 2015), 141–64.

[22] An earlier version of this paper was presented at the 'Religious Epistemology' conference held at Heythrop College, London, in July 2015. I am grateful to the audience for their feedback, and especially to the organiser of this event, Stephen Law.

Divine Hiddenness: Defeated Evidence

CHARITY ANDERSON

Abstract

This paper challenges a common assumption in the literature concerning the problem of divine hiddenness, namely, that the following are inconsistent: God's making available adequate evidence for belief that he exists and the existence of non-culpable nonbelievers. It draws on the notions of defeated evidence and glimpses to depict the complexity of our evidential situation with respect to God's existence.

The question 'Why doesn't God make himself more obvious?' is pressing for many people. Even those who trust God's self-revelation are sometimes painfully aware that his revelation is partial. Anyone whose prayers have gone unanswered or who has experienced periods of God's silence or felt absence is likely to resonate with the thought that God is hidden – even if only partially hidden. What many see of God is most like a glimpse.

But the way in which God is supposed to be hidden in the arguments under discussion in the literature on the problem of divine hiddenness is a different kind of hiddenness. This kind of hiddenness is directly related to the evidence available for God's existence – specifically, it refers to the poverty of our evidential situation with respect to God's existence. The existence of a perfectly loving God is allegedly in tension with the evidential situation in which many find themselves: the evidence, some have claimed, is not *enough* to make the belief that God exists rational, and God, it is thought, would have put us in a very different evidential situation. Our evidence would be stronger than it actually is, if there were a loving God.

My goal in this paper is to clarify this argument and point to a couple ways the argument, as presented in the literature, needs elucidation. Specifically, I want to challenge a common assumption in the literature, namely, that the following are inconsistent: God's making available adequate evidence for belief that he exists and the existence of nonculpable nonbelievers. (Throughout I will use 'nonbeliever' to refer specifically to a person who does not believe that God exists.) I conclude with the suggestion that glimpses may be a more apt analogy to use to represent our evidential situation than some of the prominent analogies in the literature.

doi:10.1017/S1358246117000212   © The Royal Institute of Philosophy and the contributors 2017

Charity Anderson

Section 1 The Argument

Most of the arguments from divine hiddenness are offshoots of J.L. Schellenberg's central argument.[1] I will be working with the following simplified reconstruction:

(1) If a loving God exists, then there are no nonresistant nonbelievers.

(2) There are nonresistant nonbelievers.

(3) No loving God exists.

In this context, nonresistant nonbelief is usually equated with non-culpable nonbelief and is characteristic of those who lack belief through no fault of their own. Nonculpable nonbelief is contrasted with culpable nonbelief. Culpable nonbelievers *resist* the evidence in some way. The existence of nonresistant nonbelievers gives rise to the problem because it is thought that a loving God would provide or make available sufficient evidence of his existence to all those who want to believe.

Philosophers have responded to this argument in a variety of ways. Some replies involve rejection of (2).[2] That is, some deny that there are nonculpable nonbelievers. This is to claim that everyone who does not believe that God exists is resisting the evidence – something akin to having one's eyes closed. Other replies to the argument involve rejection of (1). This strategy generally proceeds by offering plausible reasons God might have for permitting nonresistant nonbelief.[3] For example, some appeal to a kind of benefit that accrues to

---

[1]   See J.L. Schellenberg, *Divine Hiddenness and Human Reason* (Cornell University Press, 1993) and his *The Wisdom to Doubt: A Justification of Religious Skepticism* (Cornell University Press, 2007).

[2]   See, for example, D. Henry, 'Does Reasonable Nonbelief Exist?', *Faith and Philosophy* 18(1) (2001), 75–92 and 'Reasonable Doubts about Reasonable Nonbelief', *Faith and Philosophy* 25 (2008), 276–289, P. Moser, 'Cognitive Idolatry and Divine Hiding', in *Divine Hiddenness: New Essays*. Ed by Howard-Snyder & Moser (Cambridge: Cambridge University Press, 2002) and W. Wainwright, 'Jonathan Edwards and the Hiddenness of God' in Howard-Snyder and Moser (eds.) *Divine Hiddenness: New Essays* (Cambridge, Cambridge University Press, 2002), 98–119.

[3]   For examples of this strategy, see S. Coakley, S. 'On the Very Idea of "Divine Hiddenness": Analytic Approaches to "Apophasis"' Address at the BSPR 2015, A. Cullison, 'Two Solutions to the Problem of Divine Hiddenness', *American Philosophical Quarterly* 47 (2010), 119–134, M. Murray, 'Coercion and the Hiddenness of God', *American*

individuals when God hides himself, and others appeal to an opportunity for development that the individual would not have were God to make his existence obvious to that person.

I think this work is important, but this paper will not contribute to either of these strategies. Instead, I want to advance a different route for rejecting (1). It is usually assumed that if nonresistant nonbelievers exist, it is because God has not provided or made available evidence sufficient for belief.[4] Schellenberg maintains that a perfectly loving God would want to be in personal relationship with his creatures and that:

...seeking [personal relationship] entails the provision of evidence sufficient for belief in the existence of God.[5]

The idea is that if God makes evidence of his existence available to these people and they 'have their eyes open', they will be in a position to believe and relate to God.[6,7]

Philosophical Quarterly 30 (1993), 27–38, M. Rea, 'Narrative, Liturgy, and the Hiddenness of God', in K. Timpe (ed.) *Metaphysics and God: Essays in Honour of Eleonore Stump* (New York: Routledge), 76–96, and R. Swinburne's *Providence and the Problem of Evil* (Oxford: Oxford University Press, 1998) and *The Existence of God* (Oxford: Oxford University Press, 2004).

[4] The evidence might be publically accessible, but it need not be; it could consist of personal religious experience.

[5] J.L. Schellenberg 'Divine Hiddenness Justifies Atheism', in *Contemporary Debates in Philosophy of Religion*. Ed by Peterson VanArragon (Oxford: Blackwell Publishing, 2004), 40.

[6] Whether being in a position to believe that God exists entails that the respective individuals will actually believe that God exists is a matter that turns on certain assumptions about belief. The way I understand Schellenberg's position, he thinks that a nonresistant agent that has sufficient evidence is not only in a position to believe, but in fact believes. The assumption that the evidence will always be efficacious in producing belief is problematic for reasons Kvanvig discusses in J. Kvanvig, 'Divine Hiddenness: What is the Problem?', in *Divine Hiddenness: New Essays*. Ed by Howard-Snyder & Moser (Cambridge: Cambridge University Press, 2002).

[7] Although in this paper I follow recent literature and present the argument in a way that assumes an evidentialist epistemology, one could construe the problem in an alternative framework. One might suggest, for example, that if God exists he would make it such that each person is in a position to rationally (or safely/sensitively) believe that he exists. Whether this can

In this way, the reasoning that underlies (1) can be unpacked in the following two steps:

(4)   If a loving God exists, then he provides (or makes available) adequate evidence of his existence.

(5)   If God provides (or makes available) adequate evidence of his existence, then there are no nonresistant nonbelievers.

I will argue that on some plausible understanding of 'provides adequate evidence', (5) is false. That is, I want to suggest that nonculpable non-belief is compatible with God's providing or making available sufficient evidence for his existence. If successful, the considerations I raise undercut one route to premise (1) of Schellenberg's argument.

Two questions naturally arise when we look at the suggestion that God has not provided adequate evidence: *what exactly is God obligated to do that he hasn't?* and *what is wrong with our evidential situation?*[8] Discussions of the problem of hiddenness do not generally make clear how to answer these questions. In what follows, I examine several ways the argument and associated terminology could be sharpened.

Section 2 On 'Providing' Evidence

Consider a few statements from Schellenberg of what we would expect a loving God to do:

> God would make conscious awareness of the Divine available to every finite personal creature [capable of experiencing it].[9]

> If there is a perfectly loving God, S, unless prevented by her own culpable activity, will at all times in question find herself in possession of evidence that renders G probable....[10]

---

be done without loss of some significant features of the argument is a question I will not pursue here.

[8]   We need a gloss on 'our evidential situation' to make progress. For the most part, I will make a simplifying assumption that there is some group of people whose evidence is roughly counterbalanced for and against theism. I do this so that 'our evidential situation' refers to something close to what advocates of the argument seem to have in mind when they claim God is hidden.

[9]   Schellenberg (2007), 200.

[10]   Schellenberg (1993), 39.

If God exists and is perfectly loving, humans will be given access to evidence sufficient for belief in God's existence.[11]

Without much further explanation of what this availability might look like, Schellenberg states that:

Just by looking around us with our eyes open, we can see that this state of affairs does not actually obtain.[12]

I will suggest that to determine whether adequate evidence has been provided, we need to better understand what it is to *provide* someone with evidence.

At first glance, this might seem like a straightforward question. In fact, given the way the notion is used in the literature, one might easily get the impression that we all have a pretty good idea what it looks like. Under scrutiny, it is not so straightforward. One difficulty is due to the numerous and complex ways evidence might be available to someone.

In *The Wisdom to Doubt*, Schellenberg identifies and describes various ways evidence might go unrecognized. Among these are the following categories:

Overlooked evidence: evidence that is overlooked even though accessible.

Evidence is sometimes overlooked due to distractions or interruptions. It may also be overlooked because one simply has not directed attention to it yet. Since nonresistant nonbelievers are supposed to be individuals who have given sufficient attention to the evidence, this category is ruled out as a description of our evidential situation. That is, Schellenberg rules out the idea that God provides evidence but we overlook it.

It is worth noting that it is not obvious what constitutes sufficient attention. How easy does it need to be to take account of or appreciate the evidence? There is considerable variation on the circumstances one might be in, many of which do not fall neatly into categories. Consider a few examples. Suppose I write you a note and hide it in your house. There is a sense in which the note is available to you, though it is not easy for you to find. After looking for 20 minutes, you may get distracted. Or, you look in the wrong place. Does this count as overlooked evidence? Suppose further that I write you a

11 Schellenberg (1993), 41.
12 Schellenberg (2007), 205.

note but in a language you do not understand. You have the means to hire a translator (and I know this), but you have not found the time to do so yet. Or perhaps the letter is hundreds of pages long and you have not set aside the time to read it yet. Does this count as evidence provided? We should avoid ruling out too quickly the possibility that there are some people to whom God seems hidden but who fall into this category.

Schellenberg delineates other categories, as follows:

Neglected evidence: evidence that is accessible and failure to recognize it is avoidable.

Inaccessible evidence: evidence that has not been discovered.

Neglect of the evidence may be due to laziness or involve culpable self-deception. The explanation for why I do not have the evidence involves some failure on my part—perhaps I should have been more attentive. In this kind of situation, the evidence is available and the agent is culpable for not observing it. By contrast, when evidence is inaccessible one is in no way responsible for failing to possess it. For example, the evidence might be in a cave and no one has found it. It is possible to uncover, and we would recognize it as evidence were we to see it, but we have not discovered it.[13]

Although this discussion takes us in the right direction, these options fail to fully describe our evidential situation. In particular, the evidential situation of the group that Schellenberg is especially interested in discussing – that of former believers – does not fall into one of these categories.

Former believers, for Schellenberg, display the most disturbing type of nonresistant nonbelief: this is the nonbelief of those who regret the loss of belief and wish to regain it but are unable to do so. Schellenberg asks us to imagine individuals who:

start out assured of the power and presence of God in their lives and of their participation in a meaningful conscious relationship with God, and then they *lose* all this—often by being exposed to reasons for doubt about the reliability of the support they have for theistic belief.[14]

---

[13]   See Schellenberg (2007), 17–27 for further discussion, including further categories of undiscovered evidence and undiscoverable evidence, neither of which are relevant for my purposes here.

[14]   Schellenberg (2007), 228.

I suggest we need to consider another category: Defeated Evidence. The problem is that it is often assumed that if adequate evidence is available and an agent is not in willful resistance to the evidence, the agent will believe that God exists. But on a plausible understanding of 'available evidence' this is not the case. God might provide evidence – evidence which on its own is sufficient for belief – but one might also possess defeaters, or misleading evidence, that makes agnosticism rational despite the availability of evidence. So the dichotomy of either 'culpable resistance' or 'not enough evidence' strikes me as an incomplete description of the types of evidential situations one could be in. The epistemic situation of many people is more complicated than this.

Consider the following case where under normal circumstances we might take the evidence provided as a paradigm example of 'adequate evidence'. Suppose I have a red cup, and I want you to know that the cup I have is red. One thing I might do is tell you I have a red cup, or I might take the red cup and set it on the table in front of us, in clear view. Placing the red cup on the table seems like a paradigm example of providing you with sufficient evidence for believing there is a red cup in front of you. But consider this case where we introduce what is often called 'defeating' evidence:

Red Lighting: I place a red cup on the table in front of you. You see it clearly, but then you are told by someone you trust that the room is fixed with trick lighting – lighting which makes objects that are not red appear to be red. In fact, the testifier is mistaken, and there is no trick lighting.

Here we have the presence of evidence normally sufficient to make belief rational, plus misleading evidence. It is a common judgment among contemporary epistemologists that in cases of this sort the testimony defeats the evidence you have that the cup is red. Thus, should you continue to believe that the cup is red, your belief would fail to be rational. (Many also agree that this is a case of knowledge-defeat. That is, on the assumption that you knew *the cup is red* prior to hearing about the trick lighting, your knowledge is defeated after hearing the testimony.[15])

---

[15]   M. Lasonen-Aarnio Lasonen-Aarnio 'Unreasonable Knowledge', *Philosophical Perspectives* (2010) and Benton, M. & Baker-Hutch, M. 'Defeatism Defeated', *Philosophical Perspectives* ((2015) 29(1):40–66.) each provide useful discussions of the difficulties involved in articulating a systematic account of defeat, and also advance a minority view on which one may still be in a position to know the cup is red in cases of this sort.

One point I want to draw attention to is that the situation in Red Lighting clearly differs from a context where there is a mere absence of evidence – that is, where I provide you with no reason at all to think that the cup is red. (I neither tell you about it nor show it to you, nor give you any indication that it is a red cup.) In Red Lighting, there is some clear sense in which I have provided evidence that the cup is red. Here are a few questions we might ask about this case:

> Have I provided you with *sufficient* evidence that the cup is red?
> Are you *in a position* to rationally believe (or know) that the cup is red?
> Are you *in the presence of* evidence sufficient for belief?

It is difficult to answer these questions when your evidential situation involves defeaters. It is not immediately obvious that you are not in a position to believe the cup is red or that I have not provided sufficient evidence. We certainly cannot determine this just by looking around with our eyes open. But it seems equally clear that should you fail to believe that the cup is red, your lack of belief is not due to willful resistance of the evidence. The problem is not that your eyes are closed.

The difficulties that arise in Red Lighting also arise for some alleged cases of divine hiddenness. Clearly there are situations where agents have evidence that God exists but also have evidence that suggests God does not exist. Plausibly, God provides evidence—evidence normally adequate for belief—and agents fail to believe without willful resistance of the evidence. If such cases are possible, (5) is false.

I do not take these considerations to refute the argument from hiddenness but, rather to undercut one motivation for the first premise and to invite clarification of the argument. A few points to draw: first, we need a better understanding of the notion of providing (or making available) evidence. The literature is suffering as a result of a vague understanding of the locution. Second, we cannot reason from 'nonculpable nonbelievers' to the absence of adequate evidence. At least, this inference is not warranted without further argumentation.[16]

---

[16]   A further issue that is relevant is whether permissivism or uniqueness is correct. If permissivism is true, it may be that there is no one body of evidence such that if God to provides it to each individual, the only rational response to the evidence is to believe that God exists. It could be irrational, for some people, to believe God exists given the same body of evidence on which it is rational for others to believe God exists, if permissivism is true.

Third, there is a significant difference between an evidential situation where one fails to have evidence which, taken on its own, makes p probable and an evidential situation that involves evidence for p combined with defeaters of that evidence. The latter makes something along the lines of a free will defense plausible. Current resolutions of the hiddenness problem place the blame either on God or the nonbeliever. Either God has not provided adequate evidence, in which case God is at fault for failing to do something he ought to do, or there is culpable resistance of the evidence, which instead attributes fault to the nonbeliever. Shifting the focus to defeated evidence introduces a third option: a third party has misled the nonbeliever. (For example, a child might believe the testimony of a well-intentioned atheist family member, or a student might trust an authority figure who convinces the student that her religious experience is not to be taken seriously.)

In this way, the free will defense is relevant to the problem of hiddenness. Just as the free will of agents contributes to an explanation for why God allows (at least some) evil in the world, the free will of agents can explain the introduction of certain defeaters and thus contribute to an explanation of divine hiddenness. Of course, the freewill of agents will not explain every case of defeated evidence, since not every instance of nonbelief is due to defeaters that are introduced by agents. But insofar as the presence of evil in the world is a central source of counter-evidence against theism, and since a great deal of the evil in the world is due to the free will of agents, the relevance of free will to the hiddenness argument is significant.

Section 3 Is God Hidden? Fixing the Argument

There are various ways to understand the claim that God is hidden. If 'hidden' is taken as synonymous with 'God has not provided adequate evidence of his existence', then the reasoning above shows that the existence of nonculpable nonbelievers is not enough to conclude that God is hidden. Given this gloss on the notion of 'hidden', the following is false:

If nonculpable nonbelievers exist, then God is hidden.

One way to fix the argument is to suggest that despite the availability of evidence for belief, there is still something inadequate about our evidential situation: it is still impoverished in a way a loving God would not permit. We can ask again: *what's wrong with our evidential situation?*

One option is to argue that a loving God would provide sufficient evidence, where we understand 'sufficient' as providing adequate evidence for belief plus defeater defeaters. This initially seems to be a plausible fix. But note that this makes the argument more difficult to defend – it makes what is required of God more demanding. It might be easy to get on board with the idea that God ought to provide adequate evidence when doing so is minimal or easy. Once we introduce a requirement that God provide defeater defeaters, the demand for evidence is raised significantly.

One question that naturally arises concerns whether God is required to defeat *every* defeater anyone has. Is he obligated to make everyone's total evidence favor his existence (perhaps in a way that is obvious to each agent)? We might wonder whether this statement better captures what advocates of the argument expect of a loving God:

> (6) If a loving God exists, he provides each person with evidence that defeats each defeater that person has.

I have two worries about revising the argument in this way. One worry is that this version of the argument will strike some as less intuitive than the original argument (for the reason given above). Another worry is that there will be no limit to the amount of evidence God must provide. Notice that it is not clear what minimally I can do to get you to believe the cup is red once you believe the room has trick lighting.

Schellenberg at times uses language which suggests that he thinks a loving God would do whatever he can to ensure the belief of those seeking belief. So perhaps he would be happy with this reconstruction of the argument. But at the same time, Schellenberg maintains that he is not asking for much—nothing extreme, no compelling proofs or wondrous signs. He states that:

> ...reflection on the nature of love....[does] not suggest reasons for God to provide us with some incontrovertible proof or overwhelm us with a display of Divine glory. Rather, what a loving God has reason to do is provide us with evidence sufficient for belief.[17]

It is plausible that if providing sufficient evidence requires that God defeat all defeaters, this may result in a requirement for fireworks or something similarly overwhelming.[18] Yet advocates suggest that they

[17] Schellenberg (1993), 212–13.
[18] Imagine, for example, an individual who has been convinced not to trust religious experience but rather only to trust evidence that is 'public'

have something less than this in mind when they look for a stronger evidential position. So there is at least some cost to advancing the argument in this way, and some evidence that advocates of the argument would resist this strengthening but may be forced into it.

Another issue concerns whether there is some amount or kind of evidence God could provide that would defeat all defeaters, make belief that he exists rational, but do so without placing each agent in a position to know that he exists. One wonders, thus, whether one can avoid construing the central premise of the problem of hiddenness as follows:

(7) If a loving God exists, he would place each person in a position to know that he exists.

The line of thought in this paper leads the argument in this direction.[19] But I suspect that advocates of the hiddenness argument may not be happy with this construal of the argument.[20] The challenge then is to set up the argument such that it does not require God to place each of us in a position to know he exists, but nevertheless requires a great deal of evidence.

Regardless of whether a loving God must provide everyone with defeater defeaters—we might agree that doing so seems like a good idea—that it would be *better* if everyone had defeater defeaters, and thus it still makes sense to look for an explanation for why our evidential situation is not stronger than it is. Of course, as the literature attests, the reason might not be forthcoming. In the final section, I

---

or objectively available to many people. Suppose further that this person has defeaters that make it such that only very strong evidence would make theism probable. If God is required to defeat the defeaters of every individual in order to provide 'adequate evidence', adequate evidence may, in this case, require public signs and wonders.

[19] Note that on an E=K picture of evidence, where one's evidence consists of all and only the propositions one knows, this is a natural way to present the problem of hiddenness. Williamson advocates for this view of evidence in T. Williamson, *Knowledge and its Limits* (Oxford: Oxford University Press, 2000).

[20] There is nothing in particular that ought to dissuade the advocate of the argument from presenting the argument in terms of knowledge, beyond the already mentioned cost of demanding more of God. The reason for expecting that advocates will resist this presentation is simply that much seems to be made of God failing to meet the minimal condition of making his existence merely more probable than not for any nonresistant individual, which is quite a bit less than is required for knowledge, on most views.

will discuss one way in which thinking of one's evidential situation as involving defeaters may impact how we illustrate the problem of hiddenness.

Section 4 Glimpses

There are a number of analogies to divine hiddenness on offer in the literature. These analogies attempt to portray what God and non-believers are like. Schellenberg, the primary advocate of the hiddenness argument, compares God to a bad parent – a mother who has abandoned her child. In one picture he offers, God is compared to a parent silently watching from a distance as her child suffers and cries out, earnestly seeking the parent he believes loves him.[21] Those on the opposing side have portrayed culpable nonbelievers as analogous to people stubbornly clenching their eyes shut so as to resist the evidence that would otherwise make it obvious to them that God exists.

The analogies we use to discuss this issue are important. They prime us to see the argument in a certain light and serve as aids in making the argument more or less persuasive. When we focus on the bad parent analogy, we are more likely to be inclined to affirm premise (1). By contrast, if we think that nonbelievers are all clenching their 'eyes shut' and that getting evidence that God exists is as easy as opening one's eyes, it is much easier to deny premise (2), that there are nonresistant nonbelievers. But each of these depictions neglects an important aspect of the debate—namely, that our evidence is more complicated than this. (Note that the situation of defeated evidence is not captured by either of these images particularly well.) If in fact the evidential situation of many is mixed, our analogies ought to reflect that fact. In this way, some of the analogies in the literature fall short, and I want to suggest that we focus on a different set of analogies. By way of conclusion, I here put forward an image-type that strikes me as more adequate to the task of representing our evidential situation. (This kind of image seems to at least better depict the situation of former believers or those who have had some kind of religious experience.)

Consider glimpses. They provide the viewer with a partial vision, a glance. Glimpses are often momentary, and they are usually not

---

[21]   See Schellenberg (2004).

available on demand or at all times.[22] One feature of this kind of evidence is that in many cases it is easy to defeat. That is, while sometimes a glimpse is sufficient, given one's background knowledge, to draw a conclusion, it can also be outweighed by counter-evidence— sometimes very easily. Glimpses seem better fit to represent our evidential situation for two reasons: first, they concede that the evidence is not so clear as to make it obvious that God exists; second, unlike the image of a silent God, they represent God as having made some effort to reveal himself—while leaving it open whether he is obligated to give us more than a glimpse.[23] Analogies of this kind allow us to depict the evidential situation of the nonbeliever while maintaining neutrality with respect to the premises of the argument.

I do not mean to suggest that the analogy of glimpses will resolve the hiddenness debate. There is still ample room for disagreement regarding when glimpses constitute sufficient evidence and under what circumstances glimpses are defeated.[24] Although representing our evidential situation as similar to glimpses will not in itself resolve the issue, the image offers a more accurate representation of the complexity of our evidential situation than many of the analogies in the literature. A potential result of refocusing the central analogy for the problem of hiddenness to that of glimpses is that theists can agree that our evidential situation could be stronger than it is, without losing sight of the important point that it is not as though we have no evidence that points to God's existence. There is evidence for God's existence, even if the evidence is not as strong as we might

---

[22] Another salient feature of glimpses is the way in which they require one to rely on memory once the momentary vision is over. This makes issues relating to reconstructive memory salient to the problem of hiddenness.

[23] Has God given us glimpses as evidence? Here is not the place to argue that he has or has not – or that he has given glimpses to every individual. I will content myself to merely suggest that consideration of this image is conducive to constructive conversation.

[24] Consider, for example, Schellenberg's discussion of a case where an individual, Kim, receives a glimpse of her friend Flo at the park. (1993, 210–212) Kim is then told something that makes it unlikely that she saw Flo, such as that Flo is out of town for the week. We can easily fill in the details such that Kim will doubt that it was Flo that she saw and think it was someone else who looked much like Flo. But suppose Kim knows Flo well, and Flo was not very far away when she saw her, and it was a bright day and Kim got a clear glimpse. In this case, it seems more likely that Kim will think the testifier is mistaken.

Charity Anderson

have expected to receive, if there is a loving God. The question remains whether such glimpses are enough.[25,26]

Baylor University
Charity_Anderson@baylor.edu

[25] I am grateful to John Hawthorne and Miriam Schoenfield for discussion of issues in this paper. Thanks also to Max Baker-Hytch, Nick Colgrove, Justin McBrayer, Jon Kvanvig, Jeffrey Russell, and audiences at Oxford University and the University of London where a version of this material was presented.
[26] The research for this paper was made possible in part through the support of a grant from the John Templeton Foundation.

Misapprehensions about the Fine-Tuning Argument

JOHN HAWTHORNE AND YOAAV ISAACS

Abstract

The fine-tuning argument purports to show that particular aspects of fundamental physics provide evidence for the existence of God. This argument is legitimate, yet there are numerous doubts about its legitimacy. There are various misgivings about the fine-tuning argument which are based on misunderstandings. In this paper we will go over several major misapprehensions (from both popular and philosophical sources), and explain why they do not undermine the basic cogency of the fine-tuning argument.

Introduction

The fine-tuning argument purports to provide evidence—substantial evidence, even—for the existence of God. We think that the fine-tuning argument does exactly what it purports to do. This is not to say we think that the fine-tuning argument establishes the existence of God, makes atheism irrational, or anything like that. The epistemic status of theism depends not only on the status of the fine-tuning argument, but also on the status of just about every other argument in the philosophy of religion. The fine-tuning argument does not accomplish everything, but it does accomplish something (and that's not bad at all for a philosophical argument).

The fine-tuning argument is legitimate, yet there are numerous doubts about its legitimacy. There are various misgivings about the fine-tuning argument which are based on misunderstandings. In this paper we will go over several major misapprehensions (from both popular and philosophical sources), and explain why they do not undermine the basic cogency of the fine-tuning argument.

Overview

We have presented a more developed version of the fine-tuning argument elsewhere[1], but will give a brief review here. The standard

---

[1] See John Hawthorne and Yoaav Isaacs, 'Fine-Tuning Fine-Tuning', in Benton, Hawthorne, and Rabinowitz eds: *Knowledge, Belief, and*

doi:10.1017/S1358246117000297

John Hawthorne and Yoaav Isaacs

model of physics presents a theory of the electromagnetic, weak, and strong forces, and a classification of all known elementary particles. The standard model specifies numerous physical laws, but that's not all it does. According to the standard model there are roughly two dozen dimensionless[2] constants that characterize fundamental[3] physical quantities. Dimensionless constants specify the energy density of the vacuum, the masses of the fundamental particles, and many other things which we won't even pretend to understand properly. The point is just that our best understanding of physics doesn't only involve the simple, elegant formulae that are taught in high school physics classes and the complicated, elegant formulae that are taught in college physics classes. Our best understanding of physics also involves the specification of certain numerical quantities.

Physicists have determined the (approximate) values of the fundamental constants by measurement. (There's no way to derive the values of the fundamental constants from other aspects of the standard model. Any quantities that could be so derived wouldn't be fundamental.) Still, the underlying theory favored some sorts of parameter-values over others. A Wilsonian analysis of effective field theory[4] gave physicists a well-defined sense of what sorts of parameter-values one could expect *a priori* in a universe which has the

---

God: New Insights in Religious Epistemology (Oxford University Press, forthcoming).

[2]   A dimensionless quantity is not measured in units and thus is not unit-relative. Height, by contrast, is measured in units (inches, centimeters, and so on) and thus is unit-relative. There is, therefore, nothing particularly deep about someone being exactly one unit of height tall according to some popular system of measurement. Literally everyone is exactly one unit of height tall according to some system of measurement, and there's nothing deep about the difference between popular systems of measurement and unpopular systems of measurement. But the ratio of the mass of the proton to the mass of the electron is not measured in units and thus is not unit-relative. It would be deep if that ratio were exactly one; that would mean that protons and electrons had the same mass.

[3]   Here 'fundamental' means something like 'non-derived'. What is derived from what is obviously theory-dependent, and thus need not reflect metaphysical priority. For example, the ratio of the mass of the proton to the mass of the electron is no metaphysically deeper than the ratio of the mass of the electron to the mass of the proton. It was a matter of convention which ratio made it into the standard model.

[4]   For more about such physics, see Steven Weinberg, 'The cosmological constant problem', *Reviews of Modern Physics* 61 (1), (1989), 1–23.

sorts of general laws that our universe does.[5] Physicists made the startling discovery that—given antecedently plausible assumptions about the nature of the physical world—the probability that a universe with general laws like ours would be habitable was staggeringly low. Thus these antecedently plausible assumptions were called into question. Antecedently implausible hypotheses that afforded modest probability to this evidence from physics were massively confirmed relative to the antecedently plausible hypotheses that afforded miniscule probability to this evidence from physics. One such antecedently implausible hypothesis is that an enormous multiplicity of universes with different physical laws, a multiverse, exists. Another such antecedently implausible hypothesis is that God designed the laws of physics so as to allow for life.[6]

Most simply, the fine-tuning argument maintains that these facts of physics are likelier given theism than given atheism and thus that these facts of physics count as evidence for theism and against atheism.[7] There's much to be said about the details of the fine-tuning argument.[8] But there is also a variety of dismissive objections

---

[5]   As is customary, we individuate parameter-values somewhat coarsely to avoid triviality. Since parameter-values can vary continuously, nearly any maximally specific parameter-value must have prior probability 0. Of course, we don't actually know the maximally specific numerical parameter for any parameter, and it's easy enough to divvy possible parameter-values into equivalence classes according to their observational consequences. There's an identical sense in which someone who is a little over 7′ 9″ has a stranger height than someone who is a little under 5′ 11″, even if all maximally specific heights have probability 0. The probability of the former height plus-or-minus a nanometer and the probability of the latter height plus-or-minus a nanometer are each non-zero, making comparison unproblematic.

[6]   Our point is that this sort of divine artifice of the laws of physics was antecedently implausible, and not that the mere existence of God was antecedently implausible.

[7]   It seems plausible that the mere existence of life is a bit more probable given theism than given atheism, and thus that the mere existence of life constitutes a bit of evidence for theism. But if the fine-tuning argument is legitimate (and it is) further facts about physics constitute substantial further evidence for theism.

[8]   We've even said some of it. For more on the epistemological details see John Hawthorne and Yoaav Isaacs, 'Fine-Tuning Fine-Tuning', in Benton, Hawthorne, and Rabinowitz eds: *Knowledge, Belief, and God: New Insights in Religious Epistemology* (Oxford University Press, forthcoming) and for more on the details of the underlying physics see John Hawthorne, Yoaav

to the fine-tuning argument that should be addressed. And so we shall.

Pessimistic Induction

One popular dismissal of the fine-tuning argument relates only tangentially to the fine-tuning argument. The thought is that you don't need to take the fine-tuning argument all that seriously; there is already a heap of bad empirical arguments for the existence of God, so you can be confident that fine-tuning is just another argument that belongs on the heap. You've seen this same story play out before—is it really necessary to pay all that much attention to its latest iteration? For example, Herman Philipse writes,

> [T]heists of the past ... argued that many specific natural phenomena yield a strong confirmation of their theory, since theism allegedly provides the best, or even the only possible, explanation of these phenomena. But the history of science taught many contemporary theists that it is too risky to appeal to particular empirical phenomena in support of theism. In countless cases, scientists or scholars came up with more precise and detailed explanations of the phenomena, so that religious explanations were massively superseded. Should we not conclude by a pessimistic induction that this is always likely to happen, or that it is at least a real possibility?[9]

He continues,

> Theism will risk being disconfirmed as soon as a good scientific or scholarly explanation has been found. As the numerous historical examples show, such explanations are more empirically adequate than theological explanations, so that by now theistic explanations of specific phenomena have been abandoned massively.[10]

The general idea of the pessimistic induction is that empirical arguments for God have been bad thus far, so there's reason to discount

---

Isaacs, and Aron Wall, *The Foundations of Fine-Tuning*, (manuscript in progress).

[9] Herman Philipse, *God in the Age of Science?: A Critique of Religious Reason*, (Oxford University Press, 2012).

[10] *Ibid.*

any novel empirical arguments for God. The pessimistic induction is a fairly simple bad company argument.

Suppose we grant, for the moment, that the company of the fine-tuning argument is bad, and moreover that this bad company shows that the fine-tuning argument is similarly bad. Even granting all this it does not follow that it is proper to dismiss the fine-tuning argument. There are two kinds of bad arguments: those that give no reason to believe their conclusions, and those that give only a little reason to believe their conclusions. The former kind of bad argument warrants dismissal, but the latter kind of bad argument does not warrant dismissal. Absent a strong case that the fine-tuning argument should be dismissed, it would be foolish to dismiss it.

So should we grant that the company of the fine-tuning argument is so bad that it suggests that the fine-tuning argument should be dismissed? It seems implausible that the company is so bad—it's far from clear that the company is bad at all. There are a number of empirical arguments for the existence of God that seem to be worth taking seriously. The argument from consciousness seems very striking (and strangely under-discussed). And historical arguments are obviously legitimate—the mere fact that a religion exists is almost guaranteed to be *some* evidence that the religion is true.[11] These arguments are not failures in the sense of providing no reason to believe in theism. At most, these arguments are failures only in the sense of not providing sufficient reason to warrant belief. But it would be very strange to use that sort of failure for a pessimistic induction. (If reasons to believe in theism were piling up argument after argument then atheism would be in dire straits!)

Even granting the existence of some estimable empirical arguments for the existence of God, the overall history of empirical arguments for theism may still look unpromising for theism. Many, many empirical arguments for the existence of God have been shown to be failures. People keep coming up with empirical arguments for theism, and science keeps showing that the arguments don't work. But this whole manner of presentation is tendentious. Consider the overall history of naturalism, which looks comparably unpromising for atheism. People keep trying to provide naturalistic explanations for everything, and no matter how much they change their theories they're never able to get everything right.

The exact same pattern that looks bad for theism given one framing looks bad for atheism given a different framing. This shouldn't be

---

[11]   We assume that these historical arguments do not provide compensatory evidence against theism itself.

surprising. A pessimistic induction[12] is, after all, a kind of induction, and induction is dangerously frame-dependent.[13] All the emeralds we've seen so far have been green; naive induction would thus suggest that emeralds will be nice and green in the future. All the emeralds we've seen so far have been grue; naive induction would thus suggest that emeralds will be nice and grue in the future. But since emeralds can't say both green and grue forever, we just plain have to give up naive inductive inferences and instead actually think through what we expect to happen to emeralds.[14]

Now in the case of emeralds, it does seem that we have a nice asymmetry. Green is a far more natural property than grue.[15] But we don't think that there's so stark a disparity between the two stories we told: one in which science keeps being able to figure out more and more and another in which science keeps not being able to figure out everything.

More importantly, bad company arguments are weak. You cannot undermine a hypothesis by making myriad bad arguments for it. In general, you can put the arguments for any hypothesis into bad company, but concocting bad company for an argument accomplishes nothing.[16] The important, the proper thing is to evaluate

---

[12]   Readers are perhaps more familiar with pessimistic induction as an argument against scientific realism. We note that our contentions about fine-tuning do not presuppose realism about contemporary scientific theories, but only confidence about some of the standard model's empirical predictions. For more about the pessimistic induction against scientific realism see Marc Lange, 'Baseball, pessimistic inductions and the turnover fallacy', *Analysis* 62 (4), (2002), 281–285.

[13]   It's far from clear how one determines 'the' company that an argument keeps. It's very natural to think of any argument as keeping very different companies, and of potentially different calibers. Consider Gödel's ontological argument—what company does it keep? One natural answer is that it keeps the company of other ontological arguments, and that is poor company indeed. But another answer is that it keeps the company of logical arguments made by Kurt Gödel, and that's some of the finest company any argument could have. For more about Gödel's ontological argument see Jordan Howard Sobel, *Logic and Theism: Arguments For and Against Belief in God*, (Cambridge University Press, 2004).

[14]   See Nelson Goodman, *Fact, Fiction, and Forecast*, (Harvard University Press, 1955).

[15]   See David Lewis, 'New work for a theory of universals', *Australasian Journal of Philosophy* 61 (December), (1983), 343–377.

[16]   It is guaranteed that there are myriad bad arguments available for any position at all, so the possibility of concocting the arguments for some particular position has no evidential force.

each argument on its merits. An evaluation of an argument's company might make for a passable evaluative stop-gap, but it is wrongheaded for serious scholarship to focus on an argument's company instead of on the argument itself. There's some room for reasoning by indirections. But it's ultimately important to let each matter speak for itself. Suppose there's a student who is notoriously bad at arithmetic. You could reasonably expect the student's arithmetic assertions to be false. Nonetheless, resolute confidence that some particular arithmetic assertion of his is false should be based on an understanding of the math itself, and not merely on a low opinion of the person doing the math.

Note that the pessimistic induction for theistic arguments would look embarrassingly foolish in the face of a particularly awesome theistic argument. If we discovered the opening of the Gospel of John written onto the interior of every atom[17], it would be outlandish to remain nonchalant on the grounds that a naturalistic explanation for the writing would soon be forthcoming. If the Gospel of John were written onto the interior of every atom, atheism would look rather shaky.[18] And there's no reason to think that a pessimistic induction debunks a good theistic argument if it's an obviously inadequate rejoinder to a particularly awesome theistic argument.

God-of-the-Gaps

There is this phrase, 'God-of-the-gaps', which often comes up in contemporary arguments about religion, especially those connected to science. The clearest thing about the phrase is that it's pejorative. You're meant to accuse other people of using God-of-the-gaps reasoning, and to angrily deny that you're using it yourself. But the actual meaning of the phrase is far from clear. The idea of the God-of the gaps seems to be used to advance two very different sorts of criticisms of theistic argumentation.

---

[17]   If you protest that it doesn't make sense to have something written on the interior of an atom, we would remind you that this thought experiment involves physics working rather differently than we anticipated.

[18]   Richard Dawkins, an exceedingly staunch atheist, conceded that '[a]lthough atheism may have been logically possible before Darwin, Darwin made it possible to be an intellectually fulfilled atheist' Richard Dawkins, *The Blind Watchmaker*, (Norton & Company, Inc, 1986). And the argument from atomic inscriptions would be rather more forceful than the argument from biological design ever was.

John Hawthorne and Yoaav Isaacs

The first use of the God-of-the-gaps accusation is made by theists against other theists. In particular, the accusation is made by theists who think that there is something wrong with making empirical arguments for theism. Specifically, the worry is that if one takes some empirical argument for the existence of God seriously and considers God to feature in the best explanation for that empirical phenomenon, then when one comes across a better naturalistic explanation for the phenomenon the explanatory role for God will shrink, and that will be bad. The thought is that as we know more and more there will be less and less for God to do, until eventually there is nothing at all. Dietrich Bonhoeffer follows exactly this line of thinking,

> [H]ow wrong it is to use God as a stop-gap for the incompleteness of our knowledge. If in fact the frontiers of knowledge are being pushed further and further back (and that is bound to be the case), then God is being pushed back with them, and is therefore continually in retreat.[19]

This sort of thinking is silly. Notably, it is based on some sort of putative clairvoyance. How can Bonhoeffer or anyone else presuppose that science will eventually figure everything out? We certainly grant that it's possible that it will, but why should a theist take for granted that everything we come across in the world will make perfect sense with or without God? Science can account for more now than it could some hundreds of years ago. But this is not surprising—we didn't forget what we figured out some hundreds of years ago, and we've figured out some more things since then. These facts do not, however, provide a plausible basis for an inference that atheistic science will eventually be able to account for everything. Dismissing the fine-tuning argument out of the blind conviction that it will fall apart eventually is epistemologically risible. Maybe the fine-tuning argument will fall apart and maybe it won't. There's no legitimate alternative to thinking the matter through as best one can.[20]

Note again that this God-of-the-gaps reasoning would look foolish in the face of a particularly awesome theistic argument. If we

---

[19] Dietrich Bonhoeffer, *Letters and Papers from Prison* (Simon & Schuster, 1997).

[20] We note that it is very odd to be certain that, even given the supposition that God exists, there are naturalistic explanations for everything. Why be so confident that God wouldn't do anything that's best explained by God having done it?

discovered the opening of the Gospel of John written in the stars, it would be outlandish to remain nonchalant on the grounds that the gap in our scientific understanding would soon be filled. And there's no reason to think that god-of-the-gaps reasoning debunks a good theistic argument if it's an obviously inadequate rejoinder to a particularly awesome theistic argument.

The second use of the God-of-the-gaps accusation is made by atheists against theists. The atheistic version of the God-of-the-gaps accusation is more reasonable than the theistic version of it (though that's not much of an achievement). This accusation is that theists unreasonably take any gap in scientific understanding to constitute strong evidence for the existence of God. There's no known naturalistic explanation, so this sort of theist foolishly assumes that there is a supernaturalistic explanation.

Automatic inference from any gap in scientific understanding to the very hand of God would indeed be quite unreasonable. It is, however, far from clear that any theists actually reason in such an unreasonable way. Someone truly in the grips of God-of-the-gaps irrationality would make far more irrational inferences than anyone does. For example, until quite recently we did not have an adequate explanation for why Swiss cheese has holes in it.[21] Yet no one argued that the holes in Swiss cheese must therefore have been made by God, and thus must prove the existence of God. Everyone found it plausible that a scientific explanation for the holes in Swiss cheese was out there, even if we didn't have it yet. For another example, the phenomenon of high-temperature superconductivity is still puzzling to contemporary physicists.[22] Yet no one argues that high-temperature superconductivity must therefore be caused by God, and thus must prove the existence of God. Everyone finds it plausible that a scientific explanation for high-temperature superconductivity is out there, even though we don't have it yet. It is simply not the case that anyone thinks that any gap in scientific understanding makes for a good theistic argument. There are myriad

[21]   The theory that carbon dioxide releasing bacteria caused holes in Swiss cheese was traditional, having been first laid out by William Clark in 1917. This theory was undermined by the discovery that over the past 15 years fewer and fewer holes were appearing in Swiss cheese. There was thus a period of time in which we did not know what caused the holes in Swiss cheese and moreover knew that we did not know what caused the holes in Swiss cheese. As it turns out, the real cause is microscopic particles of hay (which became less common as cheesemaking conditions became more sanitary).

[22]   Thanks to Aron Wall for this example.

gaps in scientific understanding—scientists would be out of work without such gaps. And no one thinks there are that many arguments for the existence of God.

Admittedly, there are cases where theists fall prey to bad empirical arguments, thinking that there is good evidence for theism in areas where there isn't. In these cases, are they guilty of God-of-the-gaps? For example, advocates of 'intelligent design' contend that the development of bacterial flagella cannot be explained by gradual evolution through genetic mutation and natural selection. Isn't that pernicious God-of-the-gaps reasoning? We don't think it is. First, we're not at all convinced that there is an explanatory gap vis-a-vis the evolution of the bacterial flagellum; evolutionary biologists do have ways to account for the development of the bacterial flagellum. But suppose that evolutionary biologists had no good models for the development of the bacterial flagellum, and were merely confident that a good model was out there. Even then, the 'intelligent design' advocate would not be engaging in some distinctive sort of God-of-the-gaps reasoning. The 'intelligent design' advocate would merely evince insufficient credence that a naturalistic account of the evolution of the bacterial flagellum could be found.[23] There's no phenomenon that warrants the distinctive appellation 'God-of-the-gaps'. There's a perfectly lovely phrase for the tendency to reason in a way that illegitimately favors one's pre-existent beliefs: confirmation bias. We find it very plausible that confirmation bias is at stake in many bad theistic arguments. We also find it very plausible that confirmation bias is at stake in many bad atheistic arguments, and in many bad arguments well outside of the philosophy of religion. The term 'God-of-the-gaps' suggests that there's something special going on with certain bad theistic arguments, but there isn't.

Under no precisification of God-of-the-gaps reasoning is the fine-tuning argument impugned by it.

Frustrated Expectations

There's something potentially odd about the fine-tuning argument. We're supposed to believe that God fine-tuned our universe's parameters so that life could exist. But if God likes life so much, why did he select laws that needed fine-tuning in the first place? Why

---

[23]   See Kevin Davey, *Debating Design: From Darwin to DNA*, Edited by William A. Dembski and Michael Ruse. Philosophical Books 47 (4), (2006), 383–386.

didn't God select laws that were friendlier to life? This objection is pressed by Hans Halvorson,

> [T]he fine-tuning argument ... would disconfirm God's exist-ence. After all, a benevolent God would want to create the physical laws so that life-conducive universes would be over-whelmingly likely.[24]

Might the fine-tuning argument backfire against theism?

A preliminary qualification is called for: The fine-tuning argument really doesn't presuppose that God is interested in life. If one was antecedently certain that God would not care one whit about life but thought that God might well care about the existence of rocks, the fine-tuning argument could proceed just the same. Fine-tuning for rocks will do just as well as fine-tuning for life.[25] Additionally, there are other sorts of phenomena that are not so easily realized in other sorts of physics. Most crudely, if God wanted to provide fuel for the fine-tuning argument itself there were rather fewer alterna-tives to fine-tuning. And if God wanted both life and quasars (or some other complicated facet of our physical world) it's far from clear that there was an alternative. People talk about fine-tuning for life, but the fine-tuning argument need not presuppose that much about divine psychology.[26]

But the main problem with Halvorson's line of reasoning isn't that its conception of the fine-tuning argument is a bit narrow. The main problem with Halvorson's line of reasoning is that it has almost no bearing on the status of the fine-tuning argument. It's entirely fair to think that God would probably have created life-friendly laws. The existence of life-unfriendly laws is thus plausibly evidence against the existence of God.[27] But so what? The life-unfriendliness

[24]   Hans Halvorson 'Fine-Tuning Does Not Imply a Fine-Tuner', (Retrieved from: http://cosmos.nautil.us/short/119/fine-tuning-does-not-imply-a-fine-tuner, 2017).

[25]   Whether one is more inclined to believe in a God who was interested in creating life or a God who was interested in creating rocks will depend on one's prior probabilities in those hypotheses. For more see the sections, 'The God of Tungsten' and 'Back to Tungsten' in John Hawthorne and Yoaav Isaacs, 'Fine-Tuning Fine-Tuning', in Benton, Hawthorne, and Rabinowitz eds: *Knowledge, Belief, and God: New Insights in Religious Epistemology* (Oxford University Press, forthcoming).

[26]   It needs to presuppose a little, but not that much.

[27]   The existence of life-unfriendly laws is evidence against the existence of God if and only if the existence of life-unfriendly laws is less likely given the existence of God than it is given the non-existence of God.

of the laws may well be modest evidence against the existence of God, but if the fine-tuning of those life-unfriendly laws is powerful evidence for the existence of God, then theism comes out ahead on balance.

Consider an analogous case. Suppose that a friend of yours said that she might come by your house and write something with the leaves on your yard. Of course, your friend might not come by, and then the pattern of leaves on your yard would just be determined by the wind. Suppose that this friend is widely known to have a deep antipathy to the poetry of the 19th century. What should you think upon finding that the leaves on your yard spell out Gerard Manley Hopkins' *Spring and Fall*?[28] Your friend was very unlikely to write out a poem from the 19th century. But so what? Any 19th century poem is still *massively* more likely to have been written by your friend than to have come about by the random blowing of the wind.[29]

It's not at all necessary that the facts about fine-tuning be probable given theism. Given how fine-grained facts are, they are hugely improbable given just about any coarse hypothesis. But that doesn't matter. What matters are the comparative probabilities. If the facts about fine-tuning are improbable given theism but are vastly more

[28] Margaret, are you grieving
Over Goldengrove unleaving?
Leaves, like the things of man, you
With your fresh thoughts care for, can you?
Ah! as the heart grows older
It will come to such sights colder
By and by, nor spare a sigh
Though worlds of wanwood leafmeal lie;
And yet you will weep and know why.
Now no matter, child, the name:
Sorrow's springs are the same.
Nor mouth had, no nor mind, expressed
What heart heard of, ghost guessed:
It is the blight man was born for,
  It is Margaret you mourn for.

[29]   Note that one need not have any substantial theory of explanations in order to make this inference work. One need not claim that everything has to have an explanation nor that 'That's just the way it is.' could not count as an explanation. There might be no need to explain why the leaves spell out *Spring and Fall*, and 'That's just the way it is' might be an entirely acceptable candidate explanation for why the leaves spell out *Spring and Fall*. Regardless, that pattern of leaves is massively more likely to have been written by your friend than to have come about by the random blowing of the wind. And for our purposes the probabilities are what matter.

improbable given atheism, then the fine-tuning argument works just fine.[30]

Anthropic Complaints

There's an objection to the fine-tuning argument that goes something like this: 'The fact that we exist is supposed to be surprising evidence for theism. But the fact that we exist cannot be surprising, and so cannot be evidence for anything. If we didn't exist we couldn't possibly discover that we didn't exist. It's totally obvious that we'd find that we exist; the fact of our existence thus cannot confirm theism.' This sort of reasoning is often dubbed 'anthropic' although there are many inequivalent propositions that go by the name 'the anthropic principle'.[31]

This sort of reasoning is flawed on two levels. First, the evidence for the fine-tuning argument is not the fact of our existence. We've known that we existed for quite some time; we didn't need any contemporary physics to arrive at that conclusion. The fine-tuning argument is based on contemporary discoveries about how life is realized in our universe. It was entirely possible for us to have discovered that life was realized in some other way, in some way that did not involve fine-tuning. That was, in fact, what we were expecting. But instead we discovered fine-tuning, so now have to reckon with that.

Second, there's no principle that in order for us to have something as evidence it has to be possible to have its negation as evidence. It's possible to learn that a piece of litmus paper turned blue and it's possible to learn that a piece of litmus paper didn't turn blue. It's possible to learn that you exist but it's not possible to learn that you don't exist. It's not possible to learn that you don't exist, that you're incapable of learning, that you're completely brain-dead, and so on. But none of that matters epistemologically.[32] Anything that is likelier given theism than it is given atheism is evidence for

[30]   If one knew a conditional such as 'If there were a God then there wouldn't be life-unfriendly laws.' then the existence of life-unfriendly laws would entail the non-existence of God. Such claims are obviously tendentious, however, and are (quite properly) not generally part of skeptical responses to the fine-tuning argument.

[31]   See Nick Bostrom, *Anthropic Bias: Observation Selection Effects in Science and Philosophy* (Routledge, 2002).

[32]   A simple case: You can learn that something exists. You could not have learned that nothing exists. Yet the fact that something exists is obviously devastating evidence against the hypothesis that nothing exists.

theism. People are notoriously bad at probabilistic reasoning. We should not trust vague anthropic slogans. If you just work through the probabilities everything comes out correctly.

Unscientificness

Some people dismiss the very idea of evidence for God on the grounds that theism is not a scientific hypothesis. For example, Lee Smolin demands that any hypothesis we entertain be confirmable, falsifiable, and unique.[33] He writes,

> 'Any explanation that fails these tests should be abandoned. After all, it is possible to imagine a multitude of possible non-scientific explanations for almost any observation. Unless we accept the stricture that hypotheses must be confirmable, falsifiable, and unique, no rational debate is possible; the proponents of the various explanations will never change their minds. Yet several of the most popular explanations for the fine-tuning problem fail these tests. One such hypothesis is that there is a god who made the world and chose the values of the parameters so that intelligent life would arise. This is widely believed, but it fails the test for a scientific explanation'.[34]

Smolin's qualms are unreasonable. It's worth noting that no ordinary scientific hypothesis—no theory from the Newtonian theory of universal gravitation to quantum electrodynamics—actually satisfies Smolin's criteria. No ordinary scientific theory is actually falsifiable. You can always come up with some ancillary assumptions to save any theory you like; underdetermination is ubiquitous.[35] Additionally, many perfectly sensible hypotheses are obviously unfalsifiable. We hypothesize that the Archimedes was a fun guy to have at parties.

---

[33] According to Smolin, a confirmable theory is one that makes definite predictions that could (given favorable experimental results) redound to the theory's credit, a falsifiable theory is one that makes definite predictions that could (given unfavorable experimental results) entail the theory's falsity, and a unique theory is one such that no other simpler or more plausible theory makes the same predictions.

[34] Lee Smolin, 'Scientific Approaches to the Fine-Tuning Problem', (Retrieved from: http://www.pbs.org/wgbh/nova/blogs/physics/2012/12/scientific-approaches-to-the-fine-tuning-problem/, 2012).

[35] If Smolin said that theories had only to be disconfirmable, then this objection would not apply. But in that case he could not thereby claim that theism is an illegitimate hypothesis, as theism is disconfirmable.

Misapprehensions about the Fine-Tuning Argument

There's no possible way to falsify that hypothesis. Similarly, there's no way to falsify the hypothesis that Archimedes wasn't a fun guy to have at parties. But obviously either he was or he wasn't; Smolin's qualms would throw both possibilities away, and that's starkly unreasonable.

Note once again that Smolin's qualms would look embarrassingly foolish in the face of a particularly awesome theistic argument. If we discovered the opening of the Gospel of John written into the structure of DNA, it would be outlandish to remain nonchalant on the grounds theism is not a scientific hypothesis. And there's no reason to think that Smolin's qualms legitimate rejecting a good theistic argument if it's an obviously inadequate rejoinder to a particularly awesome theistic argument.

Measure-0 Worries

The fine-tuning argument is standardly evaluated in light of some presuppositions, namely that physical laws have the structural form that they do and that only a single universe exists. It is worth keeping in mind that, ultimately, one must drop these presuppositions and see what the evidential significance of fine-tuning is in light of the full panoply of epistemic possibilities.[36] Still, it's worth seeing how fine-tuning shakes out given the standard presuppositions. If given laws like ours and a single universe the fine-tuning argument makes a tremendous case for theism, then the fine-tuning argument should make at least a pretty good case for theism when all things are considered. And if given laws like ours and a single universe the fine-tuning argument still doesn't work, then it's doubtful that it can be made to work by dropping assumptions that are favorable to it.

The fine-tuning argument (like all empirical arguments) is based on claims about probabilities. In this case, the fine-tuning argument is based on the claim that the probability of observed parameter-values is dramatically greater given theism than the probability of observed parameter-values is given atheism. Given theism, it is supposed to be reasonably plausible that the parameter-values would permit life.[37] Given atheism, it is supposed to be wildly implausible

---

[36] At least if one wants to evaluate the overall evidential impact of the fine-tuning argument.

[37] Of course, we know more than merely that the actual parameter-values are life permitting. We have a decently good sense of what those

John Hawthorne and Yoaav Isaacs

that the parameter-values would permit life. But some philosophers (working in teams of three) have argued that this underlying claim about probabilities given atheism does not make sense. Timothy McGrew, Lydia McGrew, and Eric Vestrup and Mark Colyvan, Jay Garfield, and Graham Priest have each pressed a cluster of related worries about the probabilities invoked in fine-tuning.

One version of the worries goes like this: 'How do we get to the thought that, given atheism, the probability of life-permitting[38] parameter-values is extremely low? Well, the parameters of interest do not have maximum values; some have minimum values and others do not. That is, some parameters may take any positive real number and some may take any real number.[39] Either way, it makes sense for the parameters to take any value in an infinite range. So what probability should we assign to finite ranges of parameter-values? If the range of possible parameter-values were finite it would be natural to give every equally sized region equal probability.[40] And it still seems natural to do something like that with an infinite range of possible parameter-values. Every equally sized region should have equal probability: the probability that the parameter-value would fall between 1 and 2 is the same as the probability that it would fall between 2 and 3, is the same as the probability that it would fall between 3 and 4, and so on.

What, then, is the probability, given atheism, that the parameters would be life-permitting? The probability would have to be low—indeed, the probability would have to be 0. Life is only possible within a finite range of parameter-values. (Too much or too little of anything

---

values are—scientists can tell you the values with a modest margin for error. And the comparative likelihoods afforded by theism and atheism to such particular regions of parameter-space need not correspond to the comparative likelihoods afforded by theism and atheism to the entirety of life-permitting parameter-space. But there seems to be nothing particularly significant about the region of parameter-space in which we find ourselves beyond its life-permittingness (and rock-permittingness, and so on), so our additional evidence about what the parameter-values are shouldn't make much of a difference, if any difference at all.

[38] Again, rock-permitting would work just as well.

[39] For example, the ratio of the mass of the proton to the mass of the electron should be a positive number (at least assuming that there are no negative masses). The cosmological constant specifies the energy density of the vacuum, and could sensibly be any real number.

[40] Note that we do not endorse such indifference-driven reasoning even over finite ranges.

is bad for life.) But the value of any finite range must be 0. There are, after all, infinitely many non-overlapping regions of any finite size within the total range. They all must have the same probability, and if those probabilities were anything other than 0 they would sum to more than 1, and that's no good. So any finite region must have probability 0.[41]

But if any finite region must have probability 0, then the fine-tuning argument looks really weird. First, the fine-tuning argument wouldn't just be a strong argument for the existence of God, it would be a *maximally* strong argument for the existence of God. It's always unsettling when an argument purports to be the strongest possible argument. Even more troublingly, it looks too easy for the fine-tuning argument to be maximally strong. The life-permitting range could be arbitrarily large and (so long as it was still finite) the argument would go through just the same. You'll note that virtually no physics was required to make that argument go through, just the fact that too much or too little of just about anything and life is impossible. So it looks like the fine-tuning argument isn't a product of fancy discoveries in physics, but is instead something that would come about in any physics with parameters even remotely like ours—in those physics, just like in ours, too much or too little of anything is bad for life, and so only a finite range of any parameter-value will be friendly to life. But it's wildly implausible that such an incredibly strong argument should be so automatically available. So the fine-tuning argument must be insuperably flawed, and thus must have no epistemic significance'.[42]

---

[41]   Colyvan, Garfield, and Priest flirt with the notion that probability 0 events are automatically impossible. This is emphatically not so.

[42]   McGrew, McGrew, and Vestrup go on to note that such a probability assignment would not be countably additive, which probabilities are standardly required to be. Countable additivity requires that the probabilities assigned to countably many non-overlapping regions of parameter-space sum to the probability assigned to the union of those regions of parameter-space. The entirety of parameter-space can be divided into countably many equally sized regions (the region between 0 and 1, the region between 1 and 2, the region between 2 and 3, and so on). But there is no way for countably infinitely many regions to each receive the same probability such that the sum of those probabilities is 1. If each region receives probability 0 the sum will be 0, and if each region receives probability greater than 0 the sum will be infinite. McGrew, McGrew, and Vestrup consider this violation of countable additivity to be fatal. We are less convinced that the violation of countable additivity is fatal; there are some reasons to prefer mere finite additivity, which would not impose unsatisfiable restrictions. But our reasons for

John Hawthorne and Yoaav Isaacs

This worry is profoundly misguided.[43] It is unreasonable for philosophers to dismiss the reasoning of physicists on the basis of a misrepresentation of what the physicists say. Physicists do not claim that the probability of life-permitting parameter values is 0. The reasoning that led to the judgment that the probability was 0 was flawed and it's inappropriate to ascribe such flawed reasoning to the professional consensus of a generation of physicists. But for now we want to emphasize that the physicists simply do not claim that the probability of life-permitting parameter-values is 0. For example, physicists say that the cosmological constant (which specifies the energy density of the vacuum) is strikingly fine-tuned, that the odds of it having a life-permitting value were roughly 1 in $10^{\wedge 120}$. Physicists do not say that the cosmological constant is maximally fine-tuned, that the odds of getting life-permitting values were 0. Physicists did not come up with the

---

being sympathetic to possible violations of countable additivity have nothing to do with this case—we emphatically reject the indifference-driven reasoning which posed problems for countable additivity in the first place.

[43] McGrew, McGrew, and Vestrup write that '[t]he difficulty lies in the fact that there is no way to establish ratios of regions in a non-normalizable space. As a result, there is no meaningful way in such a space to represent the claim that one sort of universe is more probable than another. Put in non-mathematical language, treating all types of universes even- handedly does not provide a probabilistic representation of our ignorance regarding the ways that possible universes vary among themselves—whatever that means.' Timothy McGrew, Lydia McGrew, and Eric Vestrup, 'Probabilities and the fine-tuning argument: A sceptical view', *Mind* 110 (440), (2001), 1027–1038. Colyvan, Garfield, and Priest write that '[t]he fine tuning argument, on its most plausible interpretation, hence not only shows that life-permitting universes are improbable, but, arguably, that they are *impossible!*' Mark Colyvan, Jay L. Garfield, and Graham Priest, 'Problems With the Argument From Fine Tuning', *Synthese* 145 (3), (2005), 325–338. Worry about uniform probabilities is the central focus of both papers. McGrew, McGrew, and Vestrup and Colyvan, Garfield, and Priest only briefly consider the possibility of non-uniform probabilities for the values of fundamental constants, and quickly dismiss that possibility as a non-starter. Against this, it bears emphasis that such non-uniform probabilities are needed for a great deal of physics, not just for the physics of fine-tuning. For a defense of such non-uniform probabilities see John Hawthorne, Yoaav Isaacs, and Aron Wall, *The Foundations of Fine-Tuning*, (manuscript in progress).

number 1 in $10^{\wedge 120}$ capriciously; the reasoning behind that number involves seriously fancy physics.[44]

Any criticism of the fine-tuning argument that relies on arguments against assigning probability 0 to the life-permitting range of

---

[44] In particular, a Wilsonian dimensional analysis of effective field theory. We kind of know what that is. This criticism of the fine-tuning argument is not based on any understanding of it whatsoever. The rough idea of the physics is this: The values of the constants do not exist in complete isolation. The constants make contributions to the values of the other constants; they nudge each other around, so to speak. So the cosmological constant has received numerous contributions from the other constants, and physicists can know how big they are—order $10^{\wedge 120}$ bigger than the actual value. So we've got many numbers of magnitude $10^{\wedge 120}$, some positive and some negative, they get added together, and the sum is a small, positive value. Physicists did not expect that. They expected that the numbers of magnitude $10^{\wedge 120}$ would sum to something of magnitude $10^{\wedge 120}$. Trying to figure out why that sum worked out as conveniently as it did is a major project in physics. But the crucial point here is that this claim of fine-tuning isn't based on any sort of judgment that all parameter-values are equally likely. It is instead based on an expectation—an expectation rooted in a serious understanding of physics—that the cosmological constant would have a hugely different value than it does.

A toy model is helpful. Suppose that Bill and Melinda Gates decide to start living particularly lavishly, spending billions of dollars every year, buying islands, commissioning movies, and generally living it up. At the end of the year, their accountant finds something remarkable—their expenditures were almost perfectly cancelled out by the appreciation of Microsoft stock. Over the course of the year, their net worth increased by just under a dollar. It's very improbable to have the pluses and minuses cancel out so closely. Given the magnitude of the fine-tuning of the cosmological constant, it'd be more like the Gates' expenditures being almost perfectly cancelled out by stock gains 10 years in a row.

Now if there's literally no alternative account for why that happened other than that something weird happened, then there's no alternative account for why that happened other than that something of weird happened. But there are always alternatives. If someone wearing a robe had told Bill and Melinda that he was casting a spell on them to make that happen, we'd be much more inclined to believe that he was a wizard than that it was just a coincidence, and we'd be much more inclined to believe that he was running some sort of scam than that he was a wizard. But the point here is just that such near-perfect cancellation of increases and decreases of net worth are shockingly improbable unless there's something funny going on. That's exactly the kind of reasoning that the fine-tuning argument relies on, and it is beyond reproach.

parameter-values is wildly beside the point. Such criticism involves hearing a claim from physicists, disregarding that claim in favor of a dramatically different and novel claim that seems superficially similar, imputing obviously flawed reasoning as the basis of that novel claim, refuting that flawed reasoning, and thereby being confident that the initial claim was bogus. This really is as though a philosopher heard some physicists claim that there's a supermassive black hole in the centre of the Milky Way galaxy and had this response: 'Supermassive black hole? They must mean a black hole more massive than which cannot be thought. And their reason for thinking that there's such a black hole must be that a black hole that exists is more massive than a black hole that doesn't exist, thus a black hole more massive than which cannot be thought must exist on pain of contradiction. But we all know that sort of reasoning is flawed. Kant's claim that existence is not a predicate is good enough for me, and fancier work refuting the ontological argument has been done more recently. Silly physicists, getting suckered by such a well-known fallacy! There must be no black hole at the centre of the Milky Way galaxy at all'.

In fact, physicists do not base their judgments about probabilities on anything as crude as the conviction that all areas of parameter-space with equal size must have equal probability. This would be an obviously silly thing to do with parameter-space. Many of the parameters involve ratios of quantities—the ratio of the mass of the proton to the mass of the electron, for example. And there's no particularly deep reason why the parameter should be the ratio of the mass of the proton to the mass of the electron rather than the ratio of the mass of the electron to the mass of the proton—those two parameters are obviously interdefinable and equally natural. But the values between 0 and 1 in one of those parameters will correspond to the values greater than 1 in the other and vice versa. Thus the crude conviction that all areas of parameter-space with equal size must have equal probability is obviously dependent on an arbitrary decision of how to do the parameterization, and physicists know better than to depend on anything remotely like that. It is, admittedly, hard to understand the nuances of physicists' reasoning about fine-tuning. But it is not hard to understand that physicists' reasoning about fine-tuning is untouched by McGrew, McGrew, Vestrup, Colyvan, Garfield, and Priest's argumentation.[45,46]

---

[45] It is worth thinking about how to reason in contexts in which probabilities behave the way these critics have laid out—not because it is relevant to fine-tuning, but just because it is interesting. Let us therefore allow violations of countable additivity. Suppose that we know that a natural number will be generated by one of two processes, and that each process is equally likely to do the generating. The first process is not uniform and does obey countable additivity, while the second process is uniform and does not obey countable additivity. The first process will generate '1' with probability $\frac{1}{2}$, '2' with probability $\frac{1}{4}$, '3' with probability $\frac{1}{8}$, and so on. (The probability that any number 'n' will be generated is $1/2^{\wedge n}$.) The second process will generate any number 'n' with probability 0. In effect, the second process randomly selects a natural number. Now suppose that you learn what number was generated. What should you think about whether that number was generated by the first process or the second process? There's a good argument that, no matter what number was generated, you should be certain that it was generated by the first process and not the second process. After all, no matter what number was generated, the first process had non-zero probability of generating it while the second process had 0 probability of generating it. This does seem quite odd however; it seems wrong for the hypothesis that the first process was selected to be destined for confirmation and for the hypothesis that the second process was selected to be destined for disconfirmation. The unconditional probability falls outside the range of the conditional probabilities of each element of the outcome space. When this happens, mathematicians say that the distribution is non-conglomerable. Now it's well-known that violations of countable additivity can easily produce non-conglomerability, so it's not surprising that this happened in the case above. And it is not clear to us how one should reason in the case above. We are open to the possibility that one should simply follow the conditional probabilities where they lead and accept their non-conglomerability.

[46] A different—but related—worry about measure-0 probabilities is worth thinking about. Since there are continuum many possible parameter-values, the actual values are likely to have probability 0 given either theism or atheism. But probabilities conditional on measure-0 events are not generally well-defined. Colyvan, Garfield, and Priest (with something else in mind) write, 'Accepting that the universe as we find it has probability zero means that the conditional probability of any hypothesis relative to the fine-tuning data is undefined. This makes the next move in the argument from fine tuning—that the hypothesis of an intelligent designer is more likely than not, given the fine-tuning data—untenable.' Mark Colyvan, Jay L. Garfield, and Graham Priest, 'Problems With the Argument From Fine Tuning', *Synthese* 145 (3), (2005), 325–338. Happily, there are two good responses to this worry. First, it doesn't matter if the probabilities given the actual parameter-values are undefined so long as the probabilities given our evidence about the parameter-values is not undefined. And since our measuring instruments are only finitely

John Hawthorne and Yoaav Isaacs

McGrew, McGrew, and Vestrup and Colyvan, Garfield, and Priest are wrong about what the structure of the fine-tuning argument is. They mistakenly believe that the fine-tuning argument relies on uniform probability distributions over possible parameter-values. But even if one grants that the fine-tuning argument has the structure that they say it has one should not grant their conclusions about it. Given a uniform probability distribution over possible parameter-values the probability that the observed value will fall in the finite, life-permitting range is 0. Supposing that God has any non-zero probability of producing a life-permitting universe, the observed values of the fundamental constants would amount to overwhelming evidence for the existence of God. There is nothing specious about this line of reasoning. It was not inevitable that the constants would be life-permitting. The life-permitting values of the fundamental constants amount to ordinary, legitimate evidence for one hypothesis against another. It is unpalatable that such evidence would be so strong given virtually any underlying physics, and that unpalatability shows that probability distributions over parameter-values should be non-uniform. But granting the way that McGrew, McGrew, and Vestrup and Colyvan, Garfield, and Priest frame the fine-tuning argument there is no reason not to follow it where it leads.[47]

---

sensitive, our evidence is coarse-grained enough to unproblematically receive non-zero prior probability. Second, although probabilities conditional on measure 0 events are not generally well-defined, they are sometimes well-defined—and this is one of the cases in which they are. Probabilities conditional on measure 0 events are well-defined when they can be taken as the limits of continuous random variables. If you can think of a measure 0 event as the limit of other events with non-zero measure, then everything is OK. For example, suppose you have two dart players throwing darts at a continuously dense dartboard. One player, the amateur, will hit a random point on the board. The other player, the expert, will hit a random point in the bullseye. There's a sense in which the expert is no more likely to hit any spot in the bullseye than the amateur is—they each hit each spot in the bullseye with probability 0. But if you think about shrinking regions around some spot in the bullseye, the expert is more likely to get in that region than the amateur is. Because parameter-values vary continuously, even if we did know the actual parameter-values we could use this approach to keep our conditional probabilities well-defined. For more on this approach to measure-0 conditional probabilities, see Peter Urbach and Colin Howson, *Scientific Reasoning: The Bayesian Approach*, (Open Court, 1993).

[47] Fishing cases are often given as examples about fine-tuning, so we'll follow suit (though the analogy is quite rough). Suppose that—barring divine intervention—one had a uniform probability distribution over

Conclusion

The fine-tuning argument is impressively complex. A proper assessment of its strength requires a sophisticated understanding of contemporary physics, a method for reasoning about the problematic infinities of inflationary cosmology, unusually detailed credences about an unusually wide array of possibilities for physics, and general epistemological good sense to boot. We do not claim to have shown what should be made of the fine-tuning argument, but only that something should be made of it. The prominent objections to the fine-tuning argument are insuperably flawed.[48] There is no legitimate reason to dismiss the fine-tuning argument. We are left with the more difficult task of reckoning with it.[49]

University of Southern California
jhawthor@usc.edu
University of North Carolina at Chapel Hill
yisaacs@email.unc.edu

---

possible fish-widths for the finite number of fish around. According to such a probability distribution the probability that any fish will be less than a mile wide is 0. (This is an outlandish probability distribution.) Suppose one had fishing equipment that can catch any fish that is less than a mile wide but no fish that is more than a mile wide. Successfully catching a fish would then be overwhelming evidence that God graciously arranged a suitable fish; that's dramatically more likely than getting measure-0 lucky. It is, of course, unreasonable to think that catching a fish with such excellent fishing gear is overwhelming proof of God's existence, but that's only because it's unreasonable to have a uniform distribution over possible fish-widths conditional on God's non-existence.

[48]   And we don't hold out much hope for non-prominent objections.

[49]   For helpful feedback, we're grateful to Cameron Domenico Kirk-Gianni, Neil Manson, the audience at Heythrop College, and the online audience at academia.edu. This publication was made possible by the support of a grant from the John Templeton Foundation. The opinions expressed in this publication are those of the authors and do not necessarily reflect the views of the John Templeton Foundation.

For EU product safety concerns, contact us at Calle de José Abascal, 56–1°,
28003 Madrid, Spain or eugpsr@cambridge.org.

www.ingramcontent.com/pod-product-compliance
Ingram Content Group UK Ltd.
Pitfield, Milton Keynes, MK11 3LW, UK
UKHW020325140625
459647UK00018B/2017